Tripping with Na

Robin Tait is a retired academic, wl .... rn.D. in Sport Management at the University of Oregon. He has spent his professional life reading, writing, researching or teaching about sport. Robin has written three fiction manuscripts and a number of short stories. Besides sports, he is interested in travelling, and in working on his rainforest block on the Gold Coast, Queensland.

Through this book, he and his wife Valerie capture the challenges and triumphs of their life with Nathan, their profoundly disabled son.

GHB

Glass House Books
Brisbane

Tripping With Nathan

a different love story

Robin Tait

Glass House Books

Glass House Books
an imprint of IP (Interactive Publications Pty Ltd)
Treetop Studio • 9 Kuhler Court
Carindale, Queensland, Australia 4152
sales@ipoz.biz
http://ipoz.biz/

Printed in 12 pt Adobe Caslon Pro on 14 pt Avenir Book.

ISBN: 9781922830005 (PB); 9781922830012 (eBk)

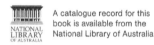
A catalogue record for this book is available from the National Library of Australia

Foreword

Come what sorrow can, It cannot countervail the exchange of joy.
– *Romeo and Juliet* 2.6.3-5

Tripping with Nathan is one of the most important books I have ever read. It's a big call but let me explain.

Nathan Runyan-Tait is a young man with severe cerebral palsy. He has a brain injury which results in very limited control of his limbs. He is unable to walk, he gets around in a wheelchair and he is dependent for all his needs on his parents and a small group of carers. Despite all of this, he is a cheerful young man, who enjoys life with his remarkable parents, Robin and Valerie. I have spent most of my professional life looking after children with cerebral palsy of all ages, all stages and all levels of severity. I thought I knew a thing or two about my job but I learnt more by reading *Tripping with Nathan* than I ever did from reading my textbooks or from my teachers. Hence the big call.

Tripping with Nathan is a heartwarming, challenging, bitter-sweet account of the challenges and rewards of being a parent and caring for a child with severe cerebral palsy. This is an epic story in four parts. It is told intelligently, with gritty realism and with humour. I laughed out loud and I shed a tear (or two).

It's not for the faint hearted but will reward the reader! Go tripping with Nathan, Valerie and Robin!

– H. Kerr Graham MD, FRCS (ED), FRACS
Professor of Orthopaedic Surgery
King James IV Professor
Royal College of Surgeons
Edinburgh, 201

Professor Graham is currently based at The Royal Children's Hospital, Melbourne

To the loves of my life: Nathan and Valerie

Contents

Part 1: Where We Are Now

Chapter 1: Departure

Fitting four people, five giant suitcases and a wheelchair into a small four-wheel drive isn't easy. OK, we have four giant suitcases and one case just slightly smaller. But there are two carry-ons as well, and they're as big as aeroplane carry-ons are allowed to be. Anyway you look at it, by the time we get all those cases, the wheelchair and four bodies into the car, we're sandwiched in pretty damned tight.

The drive to Melbourne airport is uneventful, except that the small giant, which is balanced on the back seat, keeps tipping onto Val, my wife, or the other way onto Nathan, my 17-year-old disabled son. I'm driving carefully because I don't want the small giant to tip onto Val, who'll give it to me, or onto Nathan, who can't lift his arms to protect himself, and because I don't want to have to brake suddenly and cause the top suitcase in the back to shoot forward and bang Val in the back of the head. Otherwise, it's a smooth trip, about 90 minutes, but for some reason Nathan starts getting agitated.

At the airport we have a brief argument about where to park, but there's no heat in it. We are, after all, going on a holiday for three weeks; first four days in Fiji, two days in LA, then two weeks in Costa Rica for a wedding. We park the car in a disabled parking bay where Jane is sure she'll be able to find it for her drive home.

In the short walk from the car to the airport, Nathan lets us know he is not happy. He never complains unless something is hurting, and he is complaining now. So, we don't go to the check-in first; we leave Jane with the suitcases at McDonalds and take Nathan to the parenting room to work out what is bothering him. There's a couch in there, so we're able to get him out of his wheelchair and onto the couch and search for the source of his discomfort. It's easy to find, we think.

Nathan is wearing a condom catheter, a condom with a tube that leads to a bag strapped to his leg. We haven't been using these things for long. We found out about them about a month ago, when we were looking for solutions to Nathan's unique, long distance travel problems. The problem seems to be that the condom, which is made of sticky, clingy plastic, has caught hold of some hair in that oh so sensitive place, and is pulling them hard. Ouch!

'How do we get it off?' I ask, fiddling fruitlessly with my son's abused appendage.

'Just rip it off,' says Val. 'One sudden tug.'

So, I tug, suddenly and hard, and Nathan, who is totally incapable of voluntary or controlled movement, nearly lifts off the couch. The condom holds on grimly. Bad move. My poor kid.

There's no other way but to claw, ease and bully the bloody thing off, though it brings a good tuft of Nathan's pubic hair with it. Now he's not just complaining, he's wailing.

We settle him as best we can, apologising profusely and wringing our hands at our clumsiness. Then we get him into his chair and go back to where Jane is waiting patiently at McDonalds amid our pile of luggage.

'He needs Panadol,' says Val as she delves into her handbag, 'and I need…' She turns to me. 'Go and ask for a cup of hot water and a cup of cold water.' She gestures with her head towards the McDonalds counter. This is a chore she won't do herself, and she knows that I, like her, hate asking sales staff for change, directions or anything that's not to do with them making a sale. So, she won't look at me as she throws me these orders, because she knows I'm going to be ticked. But I can't make a fuss now, my kid needs these things. I go to the McDonalds counter and get hot and cold water.

Nathan gets all his drugs, some of his food and most of his fluids through a peg in his belly. Val gives him the Panadol using a feeder tube and a syringe, and Nathan promptly throws up all over Val, Jane and himself.

There's a guy right by us in McDonalds, eating a Big Mac. He does his best to ignore us, but God knows what he's thinking.

We take Nathan back to the parenting room and discuss what to do. Not getting onto the plane is a possibility that haunts both our minds, but neither of us mentions it.

'It obviously wasn't the condom,' says Val.

'Could have been,' I reply. 'That part of the body, it's so sensitive, any kind of hurt there can make you nauseous.' I can say stupid things sometimes. When I was a kid, I got hit in the nuts by a rock in a slingshot fight with some mates, and I'm remembering that pain and the accompanying nausea as I offer this ridiculous explanation. But Val is as desperate as I am to find a solution. She accepts what I say and we decide not to abuse Nathan's penis with another condom, and to rely on his nappy until we get to Fiji.

We go back out into the real world with a thin veneer of hope that we've found the right solution. Jane tells us the guy eating the Big Mac in McDonalds had wished us good luck.

We head to a bar, for a farewell drink and to kill some time. We order three glasses of champagne, but we've hardly touched them before Nathan throws up again.

Back to the parenting room for another clean-up and a search for answers. As I'm getting Nathan out of his chair someone starts banging on the door. Val goes to the door and talks to an irate cleaner who wants to come in, and wants us out so she can do her job. She has to wait. She's not happy about it, but our ability to be sympathetic to the needs of others is low right now.

We realize now that the condom was not what was bothering Nathan, and we've got a significant problem. His eyes are glazed, but it's the nasty cough he's developing that really worries us.

A cough – so what? Nothing deadly about a cough.

Well, not usually. But Nathan only has one functioning lung; and we were told in his early years that the biggest threat to his well-being would be chest infections and lung problems. And here we are about to embark on a five-hour plane trip, with reduced oxygen levels, and our boy has a chesty cough that's bringing awful green stuff from deep in his lungs. Yeah, we have reason to worry.

Our stress levels are rising, and even though we're going, we hope, on the most ambitious holiday we've had since Nathan was born, we start to bicker, and this time there's heat in it.

We rejoin Jane and our pile of luggage. 'Should we get on the plane?' Val asks.

'Don't be bloody silly,' says Jane. 'You can get to Fiji and then see how he's doing.'

Jane is down-to-earth sensible. She has been one of Nathan's carers for a long time. She knows him almost as well as we do, and her conviction reassures us.

There is still quite a wait before our departure, and we spend most of it in line, studying Nathan for clues that will tell us how he's feeling. Val and I want to be happy about our impending holiday, but, given Nathan's uncertain state, being happy is hard.

***

Around midnight, Nathan dozes. Nathan is non-verbal. His larynx works OK, he can make noises, but we have to judge what he's trying to say by the tone of his voice more than by the sounds, and by the expression on his face. Over the years we've learnt to read those expressions. A smile means yes – and, by the way, my boy has got the world's best smile. It lights up his whole face and it causes everybody around him to smile with him. A deadpan expression means no. An *I-just-sucked-on-a-lemon* face means something is hurting. But he's asleep now, there's no point in trying to read how he's feeling; so, it's settled, we're going.

As always, we get to board first. To get Nathan from his wheelchair to his seat in the plane I have to carry him from aircraft door to seat, and every time we have the same argument with airline officials. It goes something like this:

Airline official: Sir, would you like an aisle wheelchair?

Me: No thanks, I'll carry him.

Airline official: No sir, we can't allow you to carry him onto the plane. It's a safety thing. It's for your own protection.

Me: I can't lift him out of the aisle wheelchair, it's too low and the aisle is too narrow.

Airline official: Sir, we can't allow you to carry him onto the plane. It's a safety thing.

Me: I can't lift him out of the aisle wheelchair, it's too low and the space is too narrow.

I could go on for the next ten lines and repeat the above statements over and over. This time, the airline official, a very attractive lady, who under normal circumstances could get me eating out of the palm of her hand, is unmovingly stubborn. She is not going to let me carry Nathan onto the plane.

This upsets me, but it upsets Val more. I am upset because giving in means we are going to put Nathan in the aisle wheelchair, take him to our seats, find that we cannot get Nathan out of the aisle wheelchair unless some of the seats are unbolted and removed. We will then take Nathan back to the entrance to the plane, I will lift him and carry him to the seat, which is what I wanted to do in the first place. Val is upset because the whole rigmarole of trying to lift Nathan out of the aisle wheelchair requires some manipulation of him, always unsuccessfully, by well-meaning airline staff who have no experience in handling a disabled kid. She sees it as an affront to his personal dignity. Val is big on Nathan's personal dignity.

Val tries one more time. 'Have you ever tried lifting a disabled child out of a wheelchair?' she asks. I like her *you've never walked in my shoes* strategy, but it cuts no mustard with the pretty but stubborn airline staffer.

'No ma'am,' she says, 'you have my sympathies,' – that's a line that pisses us both off, we're not looking for anyone's sympathy – 'but I simply can't let you carry your son onto the plane. It's a safety thing.'

We give in. But we don't give up, we know we're going to win in the end, and I am hoping that Pretty But Stubborn is there when that happens. We lift Nathan out of his chair and into the aisle chair, then proceed down the air-bridge and into the aircraft. We're pleased to see that Pretty But Stubborn comes with us. We take Nathan the short distance to our seats. We always ask for the bulkhead seats, because they offer more room for getting Nathan into and out of his seat, but even with the extra room we hit the standard problem: there is not enough room to stand beside the aisle wheelchair to lift Nathan out.

We look at Pretty But Stubborn to make sure she's paying attention. 'Can you lift him?' Val asks me, though she knows the answer.

'No,' I say, 'there's not enough room for me to position my feet to protect my back.'

'Can't you try?' asks Pretty But Stubborn.

'But you said using this aisle chair was a safety thing,' I argue. 'How can it be a safety thing if it risks my back?'

'I'll get you some help,' she says, and I know we're coming to the part that both Val and I really, really hate.

Pretty But Stubborn goes away, and returns with a big and burly bloke and a smug smile on her face. 'This is Phillip,' she says. 'Phillip can help you lift.'

I shake Phillip's hand, say all the right things about thanks for the help, and we've got to protect Nathan's back because he has a rod in his spine. And then together we try to lift Nathan out of the aisle wheelchair.

To understand the difficulty involved, you have to picture this scene: An aisle wheelchair takes up pretty much the whole of the aisle, with just a couple of centimetres clear on either side. To lift Nathan out of a wheelchair, seat, chair, or anything else, I have to be able to slide my arms under his body, one under the legs and one just above the hips; then – and this is the most important point – I have to be able to position the feet so I'm not leaning forward, so I can lift with my back straight and my head up. This all has to be done with me standing beside – not in front or behind – the wheelchair.

Phillip and I move around Nathan, try our hands in the right positions, shuffle our feet into the closest proximity of a lifting position that we can manage, and then stand back to review our options. They aren't very good, and both Phillip and Pretty But Stubborn now know it.

Meanwhile, outside at the departure gate, the crowd is getting restless.

'Could you lift him from shoulders and feet?' asks Pretty But Stubborn. The smug smile has disappeared. This is taking longer than she had thought it would and she is reconsidering her conviction that the aisle wheelchair has to be used.

I know how this is going to end before we try this new tactic, but I go along with it anyway. Phillip insists on taking the shoulders, as it's the heavy end and he is younger, bigger and stronger than me, and I take the feet. 'Are we ready?' I ask. 'One, two, three,' and we lift.

Nathan is 55 kilos, and that's 55 kg of dead weight; he cannot assist our lift at all. Phillip is leaning forward over the back of the wheelchair in a lifting pose that would give a biomechanist the horrors. We get Nathan out of the aisle wheelchair, Phillip is turning red with the effort, and then he and Pretty But Stubborn realise what we had known all along.

We cannot move the aisle wheelchair out of the way. It's stuck there, between the two lifters, and under Nathan's body, and there's no way on God's earth we can get it out of the way, so we cannot carry Nathan to his seat.

We carefully lower Nathan back into the aisle wheelchair. I look around for Pretty But Stubborn. I have some gloating to do, but she's done a runner.

We take Nathan back to the entrance to the plane, I lift him out of the chair and carry him to his seat.

Negotiating the narrow aisles and edging Nathan into his seat is not easy, but I manage it. I have to, there are seven plane flights on this holiday and I'll have to carry him to his seat on each one. Once seated, we have a five-hour flight with nothing to do but worry.

As the plane wings its way across the Pacific, I wind through all the things we had to go through to get here. We planned to go; we cancelled; we planned to go again. It took so much planning – how did we ever get this far?

**

Val, I should point out, is 160 centimetres of organisational dynamism. She has been planning this trip for seven months; her nephew is getting married in Costa Rica. We started out by taking Nathan to the Royal Children's Hospital in Melbourne, to hook him up to a flight simulator, to see how his lungs would respond to the low oxygen levels of an international flight. Actually, we had to do that twice, because the first time he had a cold, and when he was hooked up to the finger device that read his blood oxygen his reading was so low that the medicos refused to put him in the flight simulator. At that point, we mentally cancelled our trip, but we kept the second appointment, post Nathan's cold, and he did so well that time that we resurrected our plan.

Next in the big holiday plan we had to learn how to replace Nathan's stomach peg through which he gets all his feeds, fluids and medication. It had come out once before, and we'd had to go to the Children's Hospital in Melbourne to have it replaced. If it came out during our trip, we would have no chance of finding someone with the expertise to replace it, we'd have to do it ourselves.

And then we had to plan Nathan's diet. We have to be very careful with his diet, and we didn't want to feed him food we bought in a third world country. We decided that everything on this trip would go through his stomach peg, so we had to arrange tins of formula for peg feeds, tins of fibre booster for the formula, and feeder tubes. Finding the right formula for a kid of Nathan's size was one thing, working out how much he would need on a three-week trip was something else again.

Then there was another next, and another, and another, and another, all carefully thought through in Val's computer-like brain, with scripts for drugs and extra scripts in case the originals got lost, letters from doctors for customs authorities, solutions for bladder and bowel regulation, solutions in case of illness – which I was sure we wouldn't need – and a hundred and one other back-up plans and contingencies for taking a disabled boy on a long trip to a third world country.

Chapter 2: Fiji

At Nandi, as always, we're last to leave the plane, but this time our wait is even longer than usual. There's no air-bridge, there's a semi-long flight of stairs, and Val is bloody minded stubborn about me not carrying Nathan down them. So, we have to wait for the moveable lift, and take Nathan down in that, in a Qantas wheelchair.

This time though there is some small joy to be had in all this rigmarole. By the time I get Nathan into the Qantas wheelchair, into the moveable lift, out of the lift, out of the Qantas wheelchair into a car, been driven to the baggage claim area, found Nathan's wheelchair, got him out of the car and into his wheelchair, travelled up in a lift to Customs and Immigration, met up with Val who has exited the plane with the other passengers, we get waved to the front of the line through immigration as 'non-normal' priority passengers. Travelling with Nathan does have some benefits.

We find our bags and load them onto a trolley. It's a small trolley for such a big load, and our journey through Customs is clumsy and uncertain. Val steers the wheelchair with one hand and clutches her carry-on with the other; I push the trolley with one hand and balance the ungainly pile of cases with the other. The trolley sidles and yaws with a mind of its own and the travellers that we pass have no idea how much their ankles are in danger. Val has always said I'm a bad driver. Right now, I think she's right.

We find the counter for First Landing Resort. Our holiday is about to begin.

The wheelchair cab is nothing more than a small people mover cab, barely big enough for the three of us and all our gear.

'You must be going on a long holiday,' says the cabby, as he eyes our pile of suitcases.

'Yes, three weeks,' says Val. The cabby rolls his eyes, clearly thinking that there's an excessive amount of luggage for three weeks.

The cabby is well-meaning but overwhelmed, and it takes us a while to get everything crammed in. But eventually we are all packed and we leave the airport in a positive frame of mind.

On the way to the resort, Nathan reminds us again that he is not well. For a kid with a severe disability a cold is bad, flu is dangerous. He had pneumonia once and it nearly killed him. When we left Ballarat there was no sign of illness at all, not even a hint. Now his problem is a lung infection that has hit him like a truck. Every time he coughs, he brings up thick green muck which Val, my wife of 25 years, my delicate, blonde, blue-eyed beauty who is opposed to dirt, sweat, sport and all forms of yuckiness, sticks her fingers into Nathan's mouth and drags the vile green stuff out, while I swear that those fingers aren't ever again going to touch me until they've spent at least an hour in a steriliser.

***

The resort looks fantastic, everything a tropical resort should be. Big trees with wide, heavy leaves provide thick canopies of shade, the palm trees are heavy with coconuts, the bar is surrounded by cobbled walks and broad verandas, and the restaurant offers views of ocean and islands that could only be described as a vista.

But our room isn't ready. In fact, it won't be ready until two, and it's only nine o'clock. This news would not, under normal circumstances, be alarming, but Nathan has this cold, and his temperature is climbing, and anything that stops us getting to a place where we can deal with our crisis is significant. The warning that the biggest threat to his well-being would be a lung problem presses down on both of us.

It's hot. Until our room is ready, we're taken to what is called the day room. It's a small bungalow with a double bed. There is a cubicle with a toilet and sink where the taps don't run. We're worried about flushing the toilet, it probably won't refill. At least the room is air-conditioned. There's no room for the suitcases, which all have to stay out on the veranda with the wheelchair, so the veranda is a picture of clutter.

We change Nathan's nappy and re-apply the condom and catheter bag. Then all three of us drop into an exhausted sleep, that lasts an hour and is shattered by another bout of coughing from Nathan. Val forks the muck out of his mouth with her fingers. Whatta gal!

'Let's take a wander,' says Val, 'before we go stir crazy. 'We can check and see if our room is ready.'

It's only noon, and the room isn't supposed to be ready until two. I'm sure it won't be ready, but, in my book, noon is beer o'clock, we are on holidays, and in this resort any wandering at all will take us to the bar.

We drape a towel over Nathan's chair – the chair is black, and it's a hot and humid tropical day – get the kid off the bed and into the chair, and wander, surprise surprise, towards the bar. A sign behind the bar advertises a resort special of Bloody Marys. Sounds good; we order two; tastes terrific.

'What room?' asks the waitress. Her name tag tells us she is Leila.

'302,' says Val.

Leila looks uncertain. '302? You sure?'

'We're sure,' says Val.

Leila leaves, but she doesn't go to the cash register and she doesn't give us an invoice to sign. She comes back a minute later.

'Not 302,' she says, '101.' She gives us the invoice.

There's disappointment written all over Val's face. Can Leila see it? I sure can. I've known this woman for nigh on half my life. She quirks her lip, shrugs her shoulder, looks at me out of the corner of her cornflower blue eyes and I know what it means. Right now, there's something in her person that reads disappointment.

'But they promised us a beach front bure,' she says to Leila.

'Sure,' says Leila, '101 is beach front.'

We're both happy: Val because we've got a beach front *bure*, and me because we've got a beach front bure and because Val is happy.

'Let's go check it out,' I say.

'We don't know where it is,' says Val.

I point in the direction away from the day room where our luggage waits. 'Got to be that way,' I say. 'It's a one-oh number, and everything back that way,' I point over my shoulder, 'is two-oh or three-oh.'

The only possibility is a long, covered pathway with some exits in the desired direction. I try the first one. The short path takes me to a house that looks like something out of a glossy magazine; very plush, with swimming pool and private garden that looks out over a wide wedge of sea, sky and islands; views to die for. This can't be ours. Such luxury is not for the likes of us. I turn around and walk further down the covered path and check out the next exit, but a sign that reads Resort Employees Only tells me this is another no.

I look for Val. She's nowhere in sight. But she's got Nathan with her, she can't have gone far. I walk through the bar and down the path towards the two-oh and three-oh bureas. There's no sign of them. I'm a little perplexed.

I'm dithering at the top of the covered path when a resort employee comes of out the gate from the magazine house. 'Come sir,' she says, 'your wife is in here.'

The magazine house? We're staying in the magazine house? There must be a mistake.

I go through the gate and into the magazine house. Val is there, and boy is she excited.

'Upgraded,' she sings. 'We've been upgraded.'

'To this? You sure?'

'Yeah. Upgraded.' She can hardly keep her feet on the ground. 'Cause we had to wait so long for our room.'

I know, just as Val does, that it's not just the wait that has brought us this room – it's Nathan. Somebody in the management realm has decided to give him VIP treatment. There are advantages to having a disabled boy.

I won't try to describe the magazine house, other than to say that there's a plaque by the front door that reads:

HRH The Prince of Wales

Stayed in this Villa

On his trip to Fiji

11th. March 2005

So, assuming that HRH The Prince of Wales stayed in the downstairs bedroom, Prince Charlie and I have shared a bed.

As we move our luggage from the day room to the magazine house, our fear about Nathan's condition dissipates under the sun of our excitement, and we run around like kids in a lolly shop. My case and Val's go into the upstairs bedroom, Nathan's bags go downstairs. He needs three of the five cases to carry his clothes, nappies, drugs, tins of formula for peg feeds, tins of fibre booster for the formula, feeder tubes, syringes, leg and hand splints and the multitude of small items needed to care for a disabled boy on a holiday in Central America. All the while we're chattering like a pair of fools – about Prince Charles staying here and the private pool and garden and the outdoor shower, and about, oh boy, how we have scored.

Then we crash back to earth as Nathan starts coughing again. His mouth fills with that awful green stuff and Val's fingers go to work. She has to be quick to get it out before he swallows it and it causes him to vomit. She glances up at me. The fear is back in her eyes, and I know it's in mine too.

'Ouch!' Her yelp is testament to the danger of sticking fingers into the mouth of a disabled boy with a bite reflex and good teeth. She holds her hand up in front of my face and my stomach lurches. Her fingers are coated with this green stuff and two of them are bleeding.

'He bit me.' She doesn't mind stating the obvious.

'Go wash your hands,' I say, 'and do it thoroughly.' Stating the obvious is my forte too.

I mentioned earlier that Val is something of an organisational whizz. At home, at work, on holidays, she thinks of everything. Many of the measures that she thought of for this holiday I would have let slide as too unlikely to worry about. But now, here we are in Fiji, facing the nasty reality of Nathan with a lung infection, and Val's planning is being put to the test.

In a secluded villa, in a beautiful Fijian resort, we're close to being in paradise, but we have no time for anything but Nathan. And it is no surprise that Val's organisation is coming up trumps. Nathan's breathing is laboured, and Val dips into one of his bags for a Ventolin mask. She applies the mask to Nathan's face and delivers a spray of Ventolin into the mask. One squirt every four breaths. Four squirts.

'He needs antibiotics and Panadol,' says Val. And of course, she has them too, enough for a month-long safari. She rummages through Nathan's drug bag and pulls out a thermometer. Geez, she even brought a thermometer.

She tucks the thermometer under Nathan's armpit. His temperature is 39^0 Celsius. He's hot to the touch, his face is flushed and his lips are dry. He's breathing in short, shallow gasps. The Ventolin helps, but he still sounds like he's running a marathon.

'I wish we had a nebuliser,' Val says. 'It's the one thing I couldn't bring. I thought about it but it was too big. Maybe we can hire one.'

This is vintage Val. If I had been there without her, I would have just thought... okay, nebuliser, that would be nice, but we don't have one. But to Val, obstacles are there to be overcome not circled around. If there's a nebuliser to be had anywhere on this island, she'll find it.

Her instructions come at me like bullets. 'He needs water, he needs Panadol, and he needs antibiotics. Give him the tablets with 300ml of water. Empty his catheter bag. Check his nappy and his condom. Check the air conditioner, he'll be better off if it's a little cooler in here.' She heads for the door, and she's got that look about her that tells me that someone is going to be jumping through some hoops.

A nebuliser is an electronic pump, with a mask that goes over the mouth so moisture laden air can be forced into the lungs.

With Nathan's lungs full of gunk, it's hard for him to breathe. A nebuliser will help to loosen that gunk so he can cough it up.

With the help of the resort staff – who have no choice but to deal with her – Val tracks down a pharmacy that will rent us a nebuliser.

Meanwhile, I stand in the magazine house, looking at my son, on the first day of our holiday, and ponder the wisdom of our Costa Rica plan. The paradise outside is a distant non-reality: the sun is hot and the breeze is rustling the palm trees; the sea, the distant islands, the sky, create a picture in hues of blue. In our private garden there is a swimming pool, a riot of tropical plants, a hammock, a table and chairs shaded under a big umbrella. Outside the world looks wonderful, but right now our world is Nathan. The outside world is irrelevant.

I take a taxi to pick up the nebuliser. Fiji is green and lush, like you'd imagine a tropical island in the wet season would be. Barefoot kids pad down the rough and pitted road. Fruit vendors squat by their produce on the grassy verge. We pass through a number of small villages. The traffic is light, and the highest speed I see any vehicle travelling at is about 80 kph. The tropical air breezes through the open windows of the cab. Some of the tension drains out of me.

The cabbie's name is Buba. He tells me about his kids, about Fiji politics and about how expensive things are. He's really interested in the politics.

It takes 20 minutes to reach the township where the pharmacy is located. There's lots of foot traffic and no parking places. We cruise around the block looking for a park. I think Buba is just trying to run up the meter because we pass a number of spots. I don't mind, I'm curious about a Fijian shopping centre. Lots of small businesses, but I can't see any supermarkets or department stores.

We park close to the pharmacy, and I jump out and immediately notice that I'm the only white face on the street. This is not a point that seems to interest anybody but me.

The pharmacy is run by Indians, and the pharmacist is a tiny Indian lady with the traditional Muslim headscarf. She's very helpful, wants to know about my son, and enquires as to whether there's anything else she can do to help. Nice.

As we head back to the resort, Buba wants to know if we are making any other trips, when we're going back to the airport, and if we have transport to the airport arranged already. Then he gives me his card. 'You call me,' he says. 'I make sure you get the best price to the airport.' He taps the card he's just given me. 'Call that number. You ask for Buba. I will come quickly and give you the best price.' Then his attention changes to the rear-view mirror.

We travel in silence, then Buba says, 'My wife, she is following me. She is driving too fast.' Apparently too fast for her is not too fast for Buba.

'Does she want to talk to you?' I ask.

'She cannot talk to me. I am working.'

I look at the card he has given me. He owns the taxi company. He makes the rules.

'Do you want to talk to her?'

'No. Now is work time. I will talk to her tonight.'

We travel in silence again, until Buba says, 'She is following me. She is driving too fast.'

Buba's wife follows us all the way to the resort so I guess she wants to talk to her husband, but at the resort Buba takes off without waiting. I wonder for a moment what that was all about, then my other world reality pushes all thought of it from my mind.

We hook Nathan up to the nebuliser. It helps. It loosens the phlegm in his lungs and he coughs a lot of it up. Val is getting better at scooping the muck out of his mouth before he swallows it. Over the next couple of hours, she gets a lot of practice. His breathing eases, and he even manages to give us a tired little smile. Val and I also breathe a little easier.

Evening creeps into the sky and we wonder where the day has gone. We go to the restaurant for dinner, feeling a little better about Nathan, life, tomorrow and our Costa Rica adventure. The food is great. We get mildly drunk, and then go skinny dipping in our private pool at midnight. We are, after all, in paradise, and staying in digs that make us feel regally uninhibited.

We decide that one of us has to sleep with Nathan: me. There's no scissors-paper-rock about that decision, just Val's edict. He will need to be rolled over several times during the night to move the gunk around in his lungs. and if he does have trouble breathing, which is likely, he will need a Ventolin mask, or the nebuliser, or Panadol, or all of the above. The kid does seem to be doing better though, and we go to bed in a positive state of mind.

***

At about 4 a.m., things are not so positive. I wake from a dead sleep to find Val leaning over me and fizzing with anger. 'You careless bloody fool,' she yells, 'you're supposed to be looking after him, but look at him.'

I look. Nathan is awake, his eyes are glazed and bloodshot, he's breathing in rattling gasps and his temperature has spiked alarmingly. As I struggle towards full consciousness, he shoots a projectile vomit over Val's feet.

Nebuliser, Ventolin, Panadol, antibiotics. Keep his fluid levels up, take his temperature. Sit and stare at him and wait for signs to tell us what to do next. And that sets the stage for our second day in Fiji.

Morning comes. We are tired, but neither of us thinks of sleep. The good thing is that there are some positive signs. Nathan responds well to the combined effect of the different treatments. The muck in his lungs is not quite so thick and he's able to get rid of it a little easier, and though his temperature soars several times through the day, it comes down readily through the timely use of Panadol.

So, we're able to capture some of that holiday feeling, but Val asks me over and over, 'Should we cancel going to Costa Rica?'

Every time my answer is the same. 'No. He's holding his own. He'll be better by the time we leave.'

But it's my boy's life that's at stake here, and shadowy fears of what could happen lurk like phantoms at the edges of my brain.

He sleeps well, right through the night, and on the third day there are more positive signs. Nathan is smiling more and coughing less, and his fever stays down. The little guy seems to have a sore throat though, he doesn't want to swallow, so all his nutrition goes in via the tummy peg.

With him feeling better we're able to take in more of the paradise around us. We spend some time outside, and we're grateful for the privacy afforded by our own garden and swimming pool. Food is delivered to us from the restaurant, with enquires about Nathan's well-being from the staff.

By evening it looks like Nathan is on the road to recovery, so we go to the restaurant for dinner. The view from the restaurant is to the west, through palm trees, over the water to distant islands. As the sun slides towards the horizon, we are treated to a world of soft golden sky and brass bright water. Spectacular.

A group of musicians is preparing to play. One of them, a six-foot-four, grizzled hulk of black Fijian, comes over and speaks softly to Nathan. He leans over and gently places a kiss on Nathan's forehead. I wonder what Nathan thinks, but I also appreciate this small act of care and affection. There have been many such acts in our short stay here. To me, this one encapsulates them all.

Through dinner our discussions are dominated by our impending journey to Los Angeles. It's a ten-hour flight, and needless to say we're worried. Nathan is getting better, but the flight simulator test back in May was done on a healthy kid. His blood oxygen levels are low now because the lung infection.

Val always shows her concern by continually questioning whatever it is that we're planning. For the hundredth time she asks, 'Should we cancel our flight?'

'No,' I reply. 'He's holding his own. He'll be better tomorrow.' I show my concern by trying to overcome it, by being stupidly, blindly optimistic.

'Going to Costa Rica isn't worth our son's life,' says Val.

My response is out of my mouth before my brain is engaged. 'If I thought for a second that getting on the plane would put his life at risk I wouldn't get on the plane.'

Am I sure? I guess so. I would not, really, want to risk Nathan's life for a holiday. Anyway, he is recovering, and cancelling the holiday... well, if we're going to do that, we're not going to decide on it right now – we'll wait until tomorrow.

On our last day in Fiji, there is little should-we-shouldn't-we. The hours creep by, and no decision is voiced. We pack, and mentally prepare ourselves for the upcoming flight. I think we're a little afraid of the final commitment that would be made in voicing the question that's on both of our minds: will he be alright on a ten-hour flight? We are able to avoid it because Nathan is giving us these tired little smiles: his way of encouraging us onwards. I know Val's doubts have eased, because she doesn't ask me the *should we cancel* question every 30 minutes. I know my doubts have eased, because I'm willing to look at the reality of the situation without being blindly optimistic.

So, I guess we've decided to go.

In the afternoon we call Buba, and I take the nebuliser back to the pharmacy. In the evening he takes us to the airport. I ask him how his wife is, and then have to spend the next ten minutes discouraging him from detouring by his house so we can meet her.

***

The plane is delayed – no surprise – and as we sit and wait in the departure lounge we continue to study Nathan for clues on how he's feeling. He's not saying much, but he's more alert to what's going on around him.

Time moves on leaden feet. The building is not air conditioned. It is hot in the departure lounge, and Nathan is looking flushed and feverish. Even though we think he is recovering we are so, so aware of how tenuous his health is. And we know we are going to worry all the way to LA.

The delay drags on and on. Twice, that electric signal, that requires no words but shoots from person to person, zips around the departure lounge and a line of hot-under-the-collar passengers forms at the departure gate, only to be disappointed when an airline official informs them that the engine problem has not been fixed. The line dissipates; chairs fill; people wait.

An airport staffer gives Val a piece of cardboard to fan Nathan. A little later, a woman comes up and offers Val her spot in another part of the lounge. 'There's a faint breeze there,' she says. 'I think your little girl might be more comfortable if she had a breeze.' It's not unusual for Nathan to get mistaken for a girl. He has long curly hair and a complexion untouched by the sun, and, although he's 17, he looks closer to 13, which is kind of a hermaphroditic age in terms of appearance. We decide not to beat on the woman for calling him a her; she means well. We thank her and move to her part of the lounge, where there is a faint but cooling breeze.

Then we wait some more.

At 1 a.m. we start to board. Most of the passengers are really cranky. We're just happy the waiting is over.

We are the first ones to board. The best part about being first on is that we get to stow our carry-ons where we want to. When the plane is full, some passengers have to stick their hand luggage under their seats.

We get settled, and the other passengers start to board. There's an empty seat on my right, Nathan's on my left, Val is on his left. At home, in a restaurant, or when travelling, we usually sit with Nathan on my right and on Val's left, because I'm left-handed, Val is right-handed, and, when we're feeding him, it's more convenient that way. But this time, Val decides to sit in the seat next to the aisle, with Nathan to her right, so she doesn't have to talk to whoever has the last bulkhead seat, which is next to me. I hope whoever has this seat is going to be pleasant. It's a long flight to LA.

My travelling companion arrives, and it's immediately obvious that she is not going to be pleasant. She is in a foul mood.

Sometimes a person's mood shows from little things that you could hardly name if pressed to, but they show that a person is happy, sad, angry or whatever. This person isn't showing her mood from small signs, though there's a neon light flashing over her head that says *pissed off, pissed off, pissed off.*

She tries to cram her carry-on into the overhead locker beside mine. She shoves and wriggles and grunts but it just won't fit. She summons a stewardess. 'Isn't that too big for cabin baggage?' she demands, pointing at my bag.

'No madam,' says the stewardess, 'you may have to store your bag beneath the seats.'

Madam is not pleased. She stalks down the aisle and stows her carry-on in a locker a little removed from her seat, then returns towards me with menace in her tread.

'This is not where I wanted to sit,' she snaps. She's giving the distinct impression that the seat is unsatisfactory because it's next to mine.

She sits, then stands up and looks around with sharp, jerky movements. 'There's no television screen for these seats,' she snarls.

'Yes, there is,' says Val, and she shows the woman where the screen is tucked into the armrest. Val's helpfulness does nothing to change the woman's mood.

She sits down, and as she does so our arms brush. She grabs a cushion and wads it between us so such an obnoxious occurrence doesn't happen again. This is one nasty lady.

After take-off, the woman stands up and looks around, presumably to see if there's an empty seat somewhere so she doesn't have to sit next to me. As she stands, her mobile phone falls from her pocket to the floor. She picks it up and hurls it into the overhead locker.

In cattle class, passengers are so close to each other they can almost hear the blood pumping in each other's veins. Right now, I can feel the anger humming through this woman like electricity. Being close to such anger is not pleasant. It's going to be a long flight.

She sits down, and as she does so our arms brush again, because when she stood up the protective cushion barrier gave up its job and lapsed onto her seat.

'Oh!' The breath escapes from her mouth with disgust.

Clearly, any contact with me is like contact with someone that's got the plague, or mange. But I don't have anything nasty, except for an occasional nasty disposition, which this nasty lady is bringing on in me now. I'm not going to put up with this all the way to LA.

'Sorry,' I say.

She ignores me. Well, that's progress, but I'm not satisfied.

'Sorry,' I say again and this time my voice is louder, and she has no choice but to acknowledge me in some way. She glares at me but says nothing.

'What is your problem?' I ask.

'I beg your pardon?' she says, though she's not begging for my pardon, that's very clear.

'I said, what is your problem? You got onto the plane in a bad mood, but you've got no reason to take it out on me.' All this time Nathan and Val are sitting quietly, taking it all in but saying nothing.

The woman glares at me. If looks could kill I'd be so dead by now. Then she huffs, looks away, glares at me again and says, 'Well, thank you. You've ruined my flight.'

What planet is this lady on? I don't say anything, but I move my arm so I'm taking up the whole armrest. If she tries for a share of this thing, I'll bust her arm. Then Val calls me.

I have to surrender the armrest to lean over towards Val to find out what she wants. She wants details on what's being said between me and Nasty Lady, who, from back over my right shoulder, is glaring at me again, apparently just daring me to relate to Val about what a bitch she is. I'm about to unburden myself, when Nathan interrupts. He's hardly made a sound since we left Melbourne, he's been too sick, but now he tries to make up for four days of silence by telling us everything all at once. He talks and talks. We don't know what he's saying, but from his tone and from the smile on his face we know that he's feeling better and he's pleased about it. Nasty Lady is forgotten. A burden drops off my shoulders – and Val's – and I want to jump up and hug them both. Nasty Lady can go stuff herself. It's going to be a good flight after all.

Nathan talks for about ten minutes, and, in that time, we don't take our eyes off him, except to occasionally smile at each other. The Stewardess comes by and we order champagne. Here's to life, living, and our Costa Rica holiday which we can be excited about again.

I finish my champagne and check Nathan's catheter bag. It's

close to full. I get up to drag Nathan's bag out of the overhead locker so I can get his pee bottle to empty the catheter bag. It's just an ordinary drink bottle, meant to be inconspicuous. Then, there is a tragi-comedy moment: As I'm closing the overhead locker I drop the pee bottle, which we've been unable to clean through several fillings and emptyings, onto Nasty Lady's lap. Well, it didn't actually land straight in her lap. It hit her shoulder, then slid down her front to her lap, leaving droplets of urine in its wake. Oh shit!

Nasty Lady picks the pee bottle up and passes it to me. She gives me a weak smile. 'You'd better ask the stewards for more water,' she says. 'He won't get much of a drink out of that.'

Thank God! She doesn't know it's a pee bottle. And I am not, absolutely not, going to tell her. I take the bottle from her – I do thank her – and sit down, wondering if I'm game now to use it to empty Nathan's catheter bag and show her what the wet stuff on her blouse is. Nope, not going to do that either. I sit there with the damp pee bottle in my hands and start to chuckle. Sometimes there is such a thing as Karma.

I wonder why Nasty Lady's had a change in attitude. I mean, just for a moment there she showed an almost human face. But I don't need to ponder for long. Nathan has this one very unique ability: he brings out the good in everyone. Maybe it's because people can see his needs are greater than theirs; maybe it's because they feel sorry for him; maybe it's because they feel sorry for me and Val. I assume that, like the staff at the resort where we got upgraded, like the airport staffer giving Val cardboard to fan Nathan, like the lady offering us her slightly breezy spot in the departure lounge, Nasty Lady has seen Nathan and decided to back off and be helpful. I'm not forgiving her though. My thinking is that she would be more helpful if she backed off to the very back of the plane.

But now I've got a problem. I'm sitting with this empty pee bottle in my hand. Nasty Lady is expecting me to get it filled with water and give my son a drink; Nathan's catheter bag is full and I need to use the pee bottle to empty it; if I use the pee bottle in front of Nasty Lady... well, you get the picture. And what's compounding the problem is that it was just a few minutes ago that Nasty Lady was shooting laser-black glares at me, so trying to empty Nathan's catheter bag without her noticing is not a risk I care to take.

I peer into the top of the pee bottle, taking care not to bring it in contact with my face, then I say, in a voice that's maybe a little too loud, 'Val, there's a bug in Nate's bottle. I'll go wash it out. We can't use this bottle for drinking water anymore.' All the while I'm hoping Val's not going to look at me like I'm stupid and remind me – and Nasty Lady – what the pee bottle is for. To avoid this revelation of my deception I jump up and head for the toilets, pee bottle in hand, with Nasty Lady, I hope, thinking I've gone to clean it and Val probably thinking I'm nuts.

I come back to my seat a couple of minutes later and straight away I find, that like so often before, I've underestimated my wife. 'Honey,' she says, with wonderful round-eyed innocence, 'let's not just throw that bottle away, we can use it for other things, and we've got another bottle of water in my bag.' She takes the bottle from me, and a minute later she empties Nathan's catheter bag into it, disguised by the three seats between her and Nasty Lady.

***

The next few hours settle into the typical humdrum of a long-distance flight. Meals come and go, we sort through what movies are available and spend a couple of hours lost in those, and we nap. And all this is punctuated by whooping and hollering from Nathan. I am still so pleased about this that I want to join in with him, but I stay quiet because I'm still intimidated by Nasty Lady.

About halfway through the flight I check Nathan's catheter bag again. It's empty. Five hours, and no pee in the catheter bag? This is not good. I check Nathan's pants. They are very wet.

Now what to do? We introduced Nathan to the catheters so we wouldn't have to change him on long distance flights. In the time before we came on our holiday, when we were novices in the art of catheter and condom attachment, we had a number of condom failures and we'd thought a lot about what to do if we had a failure on one of those long flights.

We have a brief discussion. Nathan adds his opinion, at the top of his voice so all the other passengers around us hear what he's got to say. Fortunately, none of them know Nathan-Speak. We talk to one of the stewardesses, but we pick the wrong one. She's in charge of the galley and she's not interested in helping us. She insists there is nothing she can do. From long experience we know to give up on the unhelpful person and go look for another one. The second stewardess is not so dismissive. She talks to her superior and he comes and talks to us to find out what we need.

'What we need,' says Val 'is a space, with a little privacy. We can change him here on the floor, but there's no dignity in that for him, and, you know, it's not very considerate for the other passengers.' She doesn't exactly prod the steward in the chest with her finger as she's speaking, but her tone and her bearing makes it seem that way.

The steward though doesn't need a prod in the chest. He wants to help. 'So, you just need a space, to put your boy on the floor, so you can change him?'

'That's all,' says Val.

'Planes weren't designed for things like this,' he says, 'but give me a minute and we'll see what we can do.' He goes off and we talk through our options. Leaving Nathan in wet pants for the next five hours is not one of them. Neither is changing him on the floor in front of other passengers.

The steward comes back. 'There is a place,' he says, 'but there are two problems. The first thing is that it's very small.'

'If it's big enough to lay Nathan on the floor, and fit me and Rob,' says Val, 'then it's big enough.'

'You haven't heard the other problem,' says the steward. 'It's upstairs.'

The stairs up to business class in a Jumbo 747 are short, but narrow and steep. I go and look at them, so I can definitely say that I can or can't carry Nathan up them, and then I return to where Val, Nathan and the steward are waiting.

'No problems,' I say, with an optimism I don't feel. What option do I have?

I don't like to brag but I'm reasonably strong for a small man. At times like this though I worry about my bad knee and dodgy back. We explain to Nathan what we've got to do, then I heave him out of his seat. Actually, it's not that much heaving, it's more technique, and it's technique I've developed over years of lifting my boy from seats, chairs, wheelchairs, cars and various other biomechanically uncomfortable spots. When I've got him securely cradled, I head for the stairs, taking some care to get in Nasty Lady's way.

Getting Nathan up the stairs is a bit of a stagger, but, when I get to the top, I find that there's been an oversight. I should have looked at the space they offered before I carried Nathan up here. It's narrow, low and hot, a tucked-out-of-the-way little annex that's used to store the plane crew's luggage.

To make it available for us, the cabin crew have had to pull their cases out, put them God knows where till we've finished our task, then put them back. We're grateful for their efforts, we're going to use what they've given us, but I should have come and looked at it first so I could figure out the right technique for getting Nathan down on the floor in a low, tight space. Still, right now I've got Nathan in my arms, it seems he's getting heavier by the second and I don't have time for technique analysis. I bend my knees, lean against one wall and brace my feet against the other where wall meets floor, then I kind of sidle my way in. Not easy when you're carrying 55 kg of boy, but Nathan is very patient and we manage. Once we're into the annex, Val takes some of the weight and we gently lower Nathan to the floor.

God, but it's hot. The pipes on the ceiling must be hot water pipes, or maybe there's some kind of heat creation unit in the walls. It must be close to 40^0 Celsius, and the space is so small that changing Nathan is very, very hard. We try to roll him from side to side to get his wet things off and the clean ones on, but the space is so tight that it's impossible to roll him right onto his side. It's a physically difficult and exasperating task. I start to get annoyed, and Val responds by getting a dose of the giggles.

We're in a dimly lit space that's smaller than a shoe box, in a temperature that has all three of us sweating, with wet clothing to be changed and a condom to be taken off and replaced. Nothing in all of this is funny, but Val is giggling so hard there's tears in her eyes, which annoys me because I can't see what's funny and she's not helping. And then I get further annoyed when I forget how low the ceiling is, stand up and smack my head into the overhead pipes. I swear. Val giggles even harder. It takes about 15 minutes to complete the task, with a lot of frustration and irritation on my part, and no help at all from Val because she's giggling so much.

With the changing task completed, there's still a major difficulty to overcome. We have to get Nathan off the floor and back down the stairs. Getting him off the floor is hard enough. I can't get alongside him and lift with one arm under his back and the other under his legs, so we have to slide him along the floor – hard on my back and not good for Nathan's self-esteem – until we're out of the annex and the two of us can lift him.

Now for the stairs. There're only 15 steps, but they're narrow and steep, and, as I'm carrying Nathan, I can't see my feet so I have to feel my way down, slowly and clumsily, with Nathan getting heavier with every step.

We get to our seats and I unceremoniously drop Nathan into his and then fall into mine, sweating and panting. The stewardesses flutter and fluff over me, offering me water and ice and a refresher towel. They clearly think I'm heroic, and I soak up the attention, until I notice Val's look and bring myself back to earth.

Four hours and no further dramas later, the plane lands. Everybody exits. Nasty Lady doesn't say goodbye. We wait while Nathan's wheelchair is located and brought to the door. The cabin crew is pulling for us. They can't leave the plane until we do, so they're keen for the chair to be found. It doesn't take long, and we're off the plane quickly, through Customs with surprising rapidity – in spite of very long lines and seething masses of people because Nathan gets priority attention – and into another relatively short line for immigration.

Chapter 3: Los Angeles

The line we're in is for disabled people and their carers. There are nine people ahead of us, two of them in wheelchairs. The first wheelchair person has two people in attendance – it looks like a mum and dad. The second wheelchair person has five – it looks like a carer and four hangers-on. They're talking in loud voices, as if they want everybody around them to know about their holiday. I am pleased, in a very un-Christian way, when an immigration official comes and sends the four hangers-on out of the disabled line.

The carer huffs angrily, and has some words to say to the official. 'They're helping me,' she yelps. 'I have a wheelchair to take care of.' It seems nobody's told her it's the person in the wheelchair she's taking care of.

'You can have a maximum of three people for each person needing help,' says the official.

'But they're helping me. I have a wheelchair to take care of.' She thinks that repetition of the message will get the official to change his mind. Me, I'm just pleased the line in front of us has shrunk from nine to five. Then there are two. Then it's our turn.

It takes us a while at the immigration desk. Even Nathan is fingerprinted, though he's fast asleep. Then we're through, onto American soil, and a big chunk of our outward-bound travel is behind us.

We have some trouble getting a wheelchair cab. It's cold, it's late and we're tired, and when it finally arrives and we start to load the wheelchair Val gets angry because the cabby doesn't have the belts and pulleys to anchor Nathan's wheelchair in place. He's driving a wheelchair cab, for Chrissake. Surely... But we're in America, they have different rules, so I settle Val down and we accept what the cabby is telling us.

As it turns out, it doesn't really matter, because the freeway traffic is so heavy and the drive is so slow, that even if we prang it's going to be such low impact that the only casualty will be car paint.

When we arrive at the hotel, and start to unload our luggage, we see that there's a whole bunch of straps for anchoring wheelchairs, but they're in a compartment underneath our luggage. I think the cabby loaded our cases, then thought of the straps and didn't want to unload our cases to get to them.

Check-in is quick and smooth. Yes, they have our reservation, and yes, it's a wheelchair friendly room.

'Third floor, room 316,' says the clerk. 'It's our disability-friendly suite.'

The valet takes the luggage cart and we head to the elevator.

We get to room three-one-six, and see that the door is not only unlocked, it's ajar. Strange.

Val pushes the door open, and we find that room three-one-six, the disability-friendly suite, is a storeroom for beds. There's about 50 of them in there, all folded and stored end-on-end, and no mattresses. It seems that the hotel management has got different ideas about the sleeping habits of people with disabilities.

The valet calls the front desk. While he's doing that I check on Nathan. He's still fast asleep, which is not surprising, by Australian clocks it's 2 a.m. But he's had another condom failure and his pants are soaked. This gives us more of a feeling of urgency, and further shortens our patience with the hotel management.

The valet has a brief discussion with the duty manager, then he turns to us. 'Good news and bad,' he says. 'Which do you want first?'

'Bad,' I say.

'Good,' says Val.

So, the valet makes up his own mind. 'The good news is there's a suite available on the seventh floor. Room 710. The bad news is that it's not wheelchair friendly.' I think the part about not wheelchair friendly is all the bad news, but then he adds, 'and there's only one bed in there.' He should have said that there's good news, and bad news, and more bad news.

We leave the valet to care for our luggage and head down to the lobby again to fight with management.

It's a one-sided fight. They have no other wheelchair-friendly rooms besides 316, which, obviously, has not been used by anybody in a wheelchair for some time, and only one empty suite. It's room seven-ten or nothing. The duty manager apologises and offers to put a roll-away bed in the room. But, in our experiences, unless a hotel room is specified as wheelchair friendly it will be very unfriendly for wheelchairs, because there will be so little wheel-the-chair-around space. In room 710, at least the bed is king-sized, so we decide that all three of us will use that. It's been done before; in fact, I rather like it. It gives me a chance to wrap my arms around my boy and just hold him.

After changing, washing and feeding Nathan, we all sleep, for a long time.

I wake up after I don't know how many hours and check my watch. Morning – time for Nathan's drugs, peg feed, and condom check. I lie where I am and check the catheter bag. It's nearly full, that means his condom is working. I listen to his breathing. It's easy and regular, so the lung infection is pretty much behind us. I heave a sigh of relief. The day is starting on a positive note.

I get out of bed to fetch the pee bottle. It's pitch black in the room. I take a couple of groping steps and ram my toes into Nathan's wheelchair. I cuss under my breath, feel my way around the wheelchair, and stumble over a suitcase. I cuss again, louder this time. I work my way around the suitcase and bump hard into an unexpected obstacle: a cross-country buggy, beach and off-road transport for Nathan that we ordered from the manufacturer in Oregon and had delivered to the hotel. The good feeling imbued in me by Nathan's easy breathing and properly functioning condom is leaving me. I snarl at the buggy and hear a giggle from Nathan. He's not asleep after all.

There is so much luggage in the room that I have no choice but to turn the lights on, which wakes Val up. She never, ever wakes up in a good mood, and I have to put up with a spray from her on top of my stubbed toe, barked shins and lost equanimity.

With the light on, it's apparent that moving anywhere in the room could be hazardous. Moving around in a hotel room that you're sharing with two other people, a wheelchair, a mountain of luggage and a cross-country buggy is not easy. In fact, it's akin to doing an obstacle course. Val and I often laugh about what bad travellers we are because we make such a mess in hotel rooms, but we can't be messy here. There's so little space, and so much stuff to be messy with, unless we take care about where we put Nathan's drugs, our toothbrushes, the peg feeds, syringes, feeder tubes, and countless other essential items, it could take hours to find whatever it is we misplace.

We have one day in LA. The next leg of our trip is a flight to Dallas. It leaves late in the evening, and we made no plans for our morning in LA because we didn't know what state we'd be in when we got there. But, with Nathan doing well, Val decides to go shopping on Rodeo Drive. Val being your typical female, with an abundance of shopping genes, I suspect that our proximity to Rodeo Drive has had a lot to do with her LA hotel selection.

I stay in the room with Nathan. We watch NFL football on TV, drink beer and talk men's talk. I am pleased at how alert he is.

***

Val gets back earlier than expected, and Nathan greets her with a volley of noise. 'I was freezing,' she says. 'It's winter here, and look at me.'

I look. Though she looks pretty good to me – she always does, she's a snappy dresser – she's inappropriately dressed for winter, even a mild LA one, in just a blouse, short dress and sandals. No wonder she's cold.

She's also a little spooked. Some guy followed her from store to store. When she first became suspicious, she changed stores, but after two or three store changes he was still there, still pretending to be looking anywhere but at Val, but apparently following her. So, apprehension got the better of her and she high-tailed it, or rather she cabbed it, back to the hotel.

'Did you buy anything?' I ask.

'I was going to buy a sweatshirt in the Ralph Lauren store,' she says. 'It was just a white sweatshirt. I was going to buy it so I could tell people back home I bought it when I was shopping in Rodeo Drive. But I looked at the price tag, and it was $900. Nine hundred dollars!' Her shopping ethics had been violated by this outrage. 'I could buy the same sweatshirt in Australia for $100. Just a rip-off.'

She's quite deflated, but she gets over it quickly. We're on holidays and our boy is doing fine.

We go down to the bar. We're into our second round of drinks when we hear a watery tinkle. We know that sound. I close my eyes and mentally slap myself under the ear – I've left Nathan's catheter valve open. His left shoe is wet and there's a urine puddle on the carpet of the bar. Like it or not I have to be concerned with pee again. I curse myself for my absent-mindedness.

In the early hours of the evening, we start our preparations for the next leg of our travels. We have a three-hour flight to Dallas, a five-hour wait in Dallas, then five hours to Liberia in Costa Rica. Curses!

***

At LAX, the American Airlines terminal is a zoo. I've never seen so many people packed into such a small area. It's complete pandemonium. Getting through this pushing, shoving, heaving throng would be a challenge for anyone, but we have to do it with a wheelchair and a ridiculously huge load of luggage.

As we weave through an impenetrable crush of bodies our luggage trolleys teeter and sway. A number of people's angst is increased when Nathan's wheelchair barks their shins.

Val finds what seems to be the one official designated to passenger control in the whole American Airlines terminal. One person, she can't help everybody, and she is under siege from every direction as she tries to bring order to the chaos around her. But, when she sees Nathan, she recognizes him immediately as a VIP. For the next 20 minutes, she ushers Val from point to point, answering questions from irate passengers and bent on helping us to navigate the mayhem.

A security man is delegated to see us through security. Like many other officials in LAX, he is wearing a uniform bearing the letters TSA. Most of these officials look grim and unfriendly.

'What does TSA stand for?' I ask.

'Thousands Standing Around,' he says. Then he grins. 'Nah, Transport Security Authority.' He's the only one of the thousands standing around with TSA written on them that has a sense of humour.

On the flight to Dallas, we have our standard bulkhead seats. The galley for the first-class passengers is on the other side of the bulkhead. Soon after take-off the aroma of fresh baked cookies wafts from the galley and sets Nathan's mouth to watering furiously.

A stewardess comes through the curtain from first class and speaks to Val. 'Would your child like some cookies?' she asks. She has obviously noticed Nathan's VIP status.

Val flashes her most charming smile. 'He'd love some,' she says. 'But he'd also need some hot water so we can mash them for him.'

The stewardess returns Val's smile. She looks to be in her mid-thirties, and very pretty.

'No problem' she says, and returns a couple of minutes later with a glass of hot water, a fork for mashing, and two large and still warm cookies.

Whatta princess; first class in every sense.

Val mashes the cookies in the hot water and makes a dark coloured goop. When the goop is spooned into Nathan's mouth it brings a smile to his face that's bigger than the state we're headed for. But Princess Stewardess is not done yet. 'I can wrap some of them in foil so you can give them to him later,' she offers.

Chapter 4: Dallas

We get off the plane in Dallas at four a.m. and spend the next hour wandering around, looking for our departure gate and a place to change Nathan. The place is quiet. All the shops are closed, even McDonalds and Starbucks. It's a huge airport, and so spread out that it takes us a while to realise that our departure gate is in another building. That piece of information we learn from a guy driving an electric trolley with a big sign in front that says Disabled Transport. But it's not a trolley that could carry a wheelchair, and we wonder about the mentality that provides transport for some disabled people, but not for the severely disabled.

We ask another official about a place to change Nathan. He can't help us, but he directs us to an office called the Office of Special Needs.

It's easy to recognize the Office of Special Needs because it's got its name emblazoned in big letters over two very wide doors. It looks like the doors were constructed with wheelchairs in mind, and in spite of our fatigue we are cheered by the thought that this office has been set up for people like Nathan.

We enter through the very large doors and find five women in there. Two are painting the nails of another two and one is reading a magazine. They look up when we enter, but don't say anything.

'Hi,' says Val, this time using her disarming smile, 'we need some help in finding a place to change our boy. We need to take him out of his chair, and, if you have a couch or a bed, we could lie him on that would be great, but even a private place where we can lie him on the floor will do.'

There's a moment of rather stunned silence while the staff in the Office of Special Needs sum up our predicament. They look at each other, as though each one is waiting for another to offer a solution, then the woman who was reading a magazine comes around from behind her desk.

'There's parenting rooms...' she starts.

Val interrupts with a wave of the hands. 'We looked in the parenting rooms,' she says. 'They're no good for what we need. They're for parents with little babies. We can't put Nathan on a changing table that's meant to hold an infant. He's too big.'

One of the women, who is having her nails painted, says, 'Honey, if you take an elevator...' she points at a bank of elevators across the hall – I think she's pointing, maybe she's drying her nails and just happens by accident to be waving towards the elevators – '... and go up one floor, you'll find a passage to the F terminal. It's a newer terminal than this one, and I think the parenting rooms there are bigger.'

'Do you know if they have couches?' asks Val.

Five sets of shoulders shrug.

'Do you not have a couch?'

Five heads shake in unison.

We leave the Office of Special Needs and catch the elevator up one floor. As we exit the elevator, we talk about what just happened.

'What kind of special needs do they look after?' I ask.

I know Val doesn't have an answer, but then I find that the staff in the Office of Special Needs had asked themselves the same question.

After we left, they must have looked at each other, probably still with those rather stunned looks, then at the sign emblazoned over doorways promising easy access for wheelchairs, and then thought... 'Umm... Office of Special Needs... umm... maybe...' or something like that, because one of the ladies with newly painted fingernails comes running after us.

'If you'd like to come back to our office,' she says, looking somewhat chagrined, 'we think we can help you.'

Okay, it took them a moment to figure out why they exist, but then they come through in spades. They give us a room, with a table, and some cushions and a whole heap of blankets to make Nathan comfortable on the table. We are grateful, and magnanimous in our forgiveness.

After that, we have another of those long, tedious airport waits. We find a quiet part of the departure lounge and lay Nathan on the floor to give him a break from the wheelchair. We have to be careful to avoid pressure point sores on such a long journey. We lie on the floor beside him, and go to sleep as the airport stirs into life.

***

On the fourth and final leg of our journey, the plane leaves on time. Five hours and we'll be in Costa Rica. We'd get excited, but we're too tired and we all sleep until lunch is served.

For every plane trip, both to and from Costa Rica, Val has booked special food for Nathan – the food he takes orally has to be thoroughly blended – so we haven't prepared any of the liquid food that's fed through his peg. But the steward doesn't have a special meal for Nathan, and he's not interested in helping because there's no request for a special meal for Nathan on the passenger manifest.

'He just needs some soft food,' says Val. 'He's hungry. Don't you have anything that can be mashed or blended with water?'

The steward leaves, and then he comes back, but he's not carrying anything Nathan can eat. He's carrying the manifest.

'Look,' he says triumphantly, pointing to Nathan's name on the list. 'It says your son is a disabled passenger, but it doesn't say anything about special food.' He is looking unbearably smug and I am itching to punch him. Apparently, the manifest's omission of Nathan's dietary needs means Nathan doesn't get to eat.

'Isn't there anything you can give him?' asks Val.

'We have no soft food we can give her,' he sniffs.

Again, I'm within a cooee of punching him for his supercilious attitude, for calling my boy a girl, and for being such an up-himself and uncaring arsehole.

A little later, when I go to the bathroom, I see the steward at the back of the plane having his lunch. There's a big bowl of ice cream on his tray.

No soft food? What a shit-head.

As the plane descends towards the landing strip at Liberia, I think about the steward and the whole experience of our trip so far. One nasty lady, one ratbag steward, and a whole host of very helpful people. Overall, pretty damned good.

Chapter 5: Costa Rica

There is no air-bridge and no moveable lift at the airport in Liberia, so Val has no choice but to allow me to carry Nathan down the stairs. Easily done, we're still the last passengers off the plane, and the last ones into Immigration. But, even in Costa Rica, Nathan is recognized as a VIP.

We stand at the back of what looks like the shortest line. There are probably 20 people in front of us. A man with a Customs label on his vest comes over to us and beckons for us to follow him. He leads us to the front of the line, and says something to the Immigration official behind the desk. She waves us forward and we apologise to the people we've cut in front of, jubilantly present our passports, and move on to the baggage collection. Our customs friend comes with us. He helps us to collect our baggage, and then indicates that we should wait where we are.

There are no baggage trolleys like you normally find at an airport, but it's not much of a distance out to the taxi stand, and we know there's a taxi-bus waiting for us because the travel agent booked it a month ago. When we realise there are no trolleys, we figure that we can locate our driver, then ferry the bags out one or two at a time. But that turns out to be unnecessary.

Our customs friend returns, pushing a cart big enough to hold a small car. He helps us to load our luggage, points towards the exit and starts to push the cart with our luggage in that direction.

Outside the sun is very hot, an immediate reminder that we're about 10 degrees from the equator. There's a man waving a piece of paper saying *Yunyan*. Val's surname is Runyan. He must be our driver.

Our taxi-bus is quite small, and I want to take a moment to plan how we're going to get all our bags, the wheelchair, the cross-country buggy and ourselves in there. The driver though is unconcerned. He starts packing immediately, with our customs friend's help, and I ask him to wait because the first thing to go in has got to be Nathan's wheelchair, and he has to be taken out of the chair so it can be broken down so it takes up less space.

Maybe I'm tired and not thinking straight, or maybe it's that absent-mindedness thing, but when I get Nathan out of his chair – in the usual way, which means left hand under his legs and right hand behind his back – and go to put him in the taxi, I realise that I've got him back to front for a door that's on the right side of the car. I've got his feet towards the back of the seat and his head where his feet should be.

Then helpful hands come from everywhere, and I have to wonder how many people at the airport have nothing else to do but help needy tourists. Kids, adolescents, adults, all arrive out of nowhere, all talking, pointing, giving orders. Two kids scramble into the back of the taxi and lean over the seat to try and take some of Nathan's weight so he can be turned around. Another two people get into the front doors and climb over the seats to help by turning him from there. When Nathan gets deposited in his seat, I do a quick count. I think there are seven people involved in the final depositing. Others poke their heads in windows and offer streams of advice. They're speaking in Spanish so I don't know if it's good advice or not. I have no idea who all these people are, or what their role at the airport is, but right now, as far as they're concerned, their job is to help Nathan.

My boy, he has VIP written all over him.

We get Nathan into his seat, and our audience turns its attention to our luggage. Bags, buggy, cases and chair are tried in various places. We pack, unpack, repack. Then we're ready to roll.

Door's slam. Val leans out the window and blows our helping crowd a kiss. As the taxi starts to move, I look out of the back window. The crowd of helpers is standing in the road and waving. Some of them are waving with two hands. I wonder if that's a Costa Rica thing.

We pull out onto the main road. We're here. We made it. If we can travel all this way to a third world country, we can go anywhere.

Mind you, it wasn't always so easy.

Part 2: Where We Came From

Chapter 6: About Us

It is hard, very hard, for parents when they find their newborn is disabled. One of the things that made it hard for me was that I was so, so into sport, and I absolutely knew that my son was going to be a champion. And it was no easier for Val. She's not into sport but she is a perfectionist. Where I saw the fruit of my loins as a future gold medal earner, Val was just as sure that he would be a winner, whatever the path he took through life.

I started my professional life as a physical education teacher in Broken Hill. I loved it. I was young, into all forms of physical activity and the pub life. Born and raised a small-town boy I never wanted to live in a big city, and here I was in a town of 30,000, with 28 pubs and eight (I think) licensed clubs. A town where the social life largely revolved around sport. I was there for five years, loved every minute, but after five years I was ready for a change.

A change had to involve more than just going to a new town in the same state and teaching physical education again. I wanted a real change, and that meant going overseas. With little money to bankroll my travels my options were to go overseas and teach, or go overseas and study. I chose to go overseas and study.

For those that knew me well it probably looked like an odd decision. Through primary school, high school, teachers' college, I had always been a drop kick of a student. So why would I choose to pursue something I wasn't any good at?

Because I had been no good at it, that was the basic reason. Going overseas to study would be my chance for atonement. And, further, I saw overseas study as a launching pad for further travel. I planned to complete my degree and then go where the wind took me, and as long as it was new and different I didn't much care where that was.

But then a strange thing happened.

When I got to the US, I found that I was good, or at least capable, at the studying thing, though at the start I had little faith in myself. I remember sitting on my bed in the dorms at the university in Kansas, on the morning of the first day of classes, and looking at the semester's study material. It looked scary, and I was asking myself why I had chosen to go back into academia when I had always been such a bad student. My conversation with myself ran something like this:

You must be nuts.

No, I'm not nuts. I can do it. I've just never tried properly before.

What? Six years of primary school and six years… no, seven – you repeated the final year of high school – and you couldn't get it right. And then three years of teachers' college where you languished in the bottom ten percent every year. It's not that you didn't try, it's just that you're no bloody good at studying.

I've never really tried. I won't know if I'm any good if I don't give it one last 'damn-the-torpedoes-full-speed-ahead' try.

Give up now. Save yourself the heartache. You're no good at this.

I've got to try. This is my last chance.

But you—

Then I told myself to shut up and went off to class.

Treating it as my last chance, being a little older and, I would hope, a little more mature, I found that academic success came quite easily. I organised myself, I prioritised my time, and I got good grades right from the start. I didn't live a monastic life, I partied, played rugby, worked part-time and enjoyed myself; and I got good grades. I enjoyed myself so much that, when I was finishing my undergraduate degree, I told myself that this was good, I should spend another year in academia and do a Master's degree. And when I was finishing that, I told myself that this was good, I should spend a bit more time in academia and do a doctoral degree.

This would be, I told myself, just a short-term delay of my plan to cast my fate to the winds and travel, travel, travel. I applied for scholarships at several universities, got a few offers, and accepted one from the University of Oregon where I would earn my keep as an assistant volleyball coach.

***

The University of Oregon is in Eugene, a pretty town, but I didn't enjoy the first couple of years. My biggest problem was an unhappy relationship. I met Kim in the first month, fell for her head-over-heels and kept falling. I was so in love that I didn't see it when the relationship turned bad, and when she graduated and moved away, I missed her terribly. Everywhere I went I was reminded of her. I was miserable. I believed that I couldn't get out of Eugene fast enough.

But, after a short time, with her gone, life started to be enjoyable again.

My lesser problem was that I had trouble finding an area of expertise in my Ph.D. program. In the end, I kind of fell into sport management. It was a de facto choice, because the science subjects scared me so much, I avoided them wherever possible. I nearly quit a few times, but – alright, somewhere in this story I should be allowed a warm fuzzy – I'm not that big on quitting, so I stuck with it, in the face of renewed self-doubts about my academic capabilities.

The volleyball coaching turned into something of a washout. The first year was good, but in the second year there was a new head coach, and she and I didn't get on. Besides that, my unhappy relationship with Kim was at the intense, volatile, and untrusting stage and it was messing badly with my head. An unhappy person cannot be a good coach, in any sport let alone in one as team-oriented as volleyball, so I quit coaching volleyball and spent the next year working in the university's intramural sports office. But I wasn't into it, I didn't do that well, and at the end of the year my scholarship was not renewed.

Let's go back to where we started this chapter, when I was in the world's top ten percent of lousy students. In those days I had developed some bad habits that were not easy to get rid of. Like partying on week nights when there was studying to be done; chasing women instead of chasing good grades; keeping rugby higher on the priority list than studying. When I got to Oregon, I hung onto some of these bad habits – I guess didn't want to get rid of them – and, in a Ph.D. program, bad habits are fatal.

A Ph.D. program at the University of Oregon was serious business. It involved serious hard work and serious research. I managed, but I didn't shine, and when my scholarship finished – it was a three-year scholarship, ample time to finish a Ph.D. if you apply yourself properly, which I didn't – I had to seek alternative employment. And that brought me to Old Taylor's Bar, to one of the happiest periods of my life, and, eventually, to my future wife Valerie.

***

Old Taylor's Bar was a grungy, down-at-the-heel place, right opposite the university bookshop on one of the busiest corners in the university precinct. It was a popular student hang-out. I had been working there for about six months when I met Valerie.

It was summer. There weren't many students around. The university was quiet and Taylor's, every day and every night, was quieter. Eugene is known for its wet weather, but I remember this as being a warm, still and beautiful day. Maybe I've idealised it a little, but as I went in to work it was a golden evening, with the birds singing in trees that were heavy with leaf. My world was contented and peaceful. I checked in for work at eight o'clock. Todd, one of the owners, was in charge and I was the only other worker. There weren't many customers, and not much work was being done. Todd was an amiable bloke, as likely to do a chore himself as to ask one of his employees to do it. We were both pretty much just killing time when this friend of mine came in. And she had someone with her.

My friend's companion perched herself on a bar stool. Her name was Valerie, she was a trainee stockbroker, and she lived in Portland. She was small and slender, very shapely, with long blonde hair that cascaded around an oval face like a curly yellow waterfall. And her eyes were so blue. Framed by that blonde mane they were like cornflowers in a field of wheat. She looked like a fairy princess. My friends later knick-named her Guinevere.

It would be trite of me to say that we weren't all that serious in the beginning. Serious was not on either of our minds, but we gradually moved that way, and before I knew it, she was too much a part of my life for me to lose. For the first six months of our relationship, she travelled down from Portland almost every week. It was a 240-mile round trip, but I never once heard her complain about it. She turned up regularly because she was, then as she is now, a loyal little soul.

For the next six months, she still came down most weekends, but occasionally I would find a ride up to Portland and stay at her place. She lived with her mother. Her mother was not happy about our relationship, so staying there wasn't always a comfortable experience.

***

I actually shocked myself when I started to think of our relationship in terms of permanency. I was in my early 30s, commitment-shy, having the time of my life. Why would I want things to change?

Because, like it or not, they were going to.

Val lived a 120 miles away. She had a high-pressure job that would eventually consume a big chunk of her time and energy. She had a mother that was in her ear, pretty much continually, telling her that I was too old, no good, Val should think about all the women I had been with.

And on top of that, Valerie was a gorgeous little lady: 22 years old, with blonde hair, blue-eyes and with a face and figure that turned heads wherever she went. If I didn't offer her some kind of commitment, I would eventually lose her to distance, job, mother's anti-Robin campaign and other men.

As our relationship meandered happily along, I started thinking of the future and pondering my options. I was living one of the best ever periods of my life, but I'd nearly finished my Ph.D., and when I finished studying my visa would expire. I was working in a bar which, whereas it was fun, paid shit and was not a long-term employment option. Whichever way I looked at it everything about my life was temporary. Except for Val, who I wanted to hold on to, so I decided to propose.

I made this decision on a Thursday. Val arrived, as usual, around 5 p.m. the next day. She has told me numerous times since then that, when she came down that weekend, she intended to break up with me because she didn't think the relationship was going to progress, but she reckons I got in first with the proposal. We'd gone out for Chinese food, I proposed and she used the tension of the moment to get all the prawns in the sweet and sour dish we'd ordered. She kept me hanging for a while, and when she'd eaten all the prawns, she accepted my proposal.

When she went home on Sunday night, she told her mother she was getting married.

Her mother was not happy. 'Who to?' she asked.

We set the wedding date for six months hence, in early December, and we planned to move to Australia shortly after that. When the planning got down to the fine details, *shortly after that* turned out to be three weeks after the wedding.

The wedding was on a Sunday. On the day before, I played in the last game of the rugby season; my last game for the University of Oregon. The game was against Eugene Rugby Club, our traditional rival. They were, like us, undefeated coming into that game. Think about it: two undefeated teams, traditional rivals, playing each other in the last game of the season; my last game after five years, and I'm getting married the next day.

We won by nine points.

Fairytale ending?

You bet!

***

We had known each other for 18 months when we got married. The ceremony was at a church in Lake Oswego. We made the place famous. Bruce Springsteen got married there a couple of years later.

I don't remember too much about the night before the wedding, not because I got wildly drunk, but because I was so overwhelmed by the fact that I was getting married that I was

50

in a haze of bewilderment. I didn't play up, get drunk or wild or crazy, and I probably wasn't very good company. All I could think about was what was to happen the next day. I was subdued, preoccupied, and, truth to tell, scared shitless. I thought a few times about doing a runner, but I didn't have the nerve.

There were a lot of people at the wedding; more people, in fact, than we invited. My whole rugby team turned up, even the ones who didn't like me. I think the entire crew from Taylors came too, though, also, some of them hadn't been invited. I still wonder who ran the bar that night.

From the time we got married, until we left for Australia, we stayed at Val's mum's place in Lake Oswego. The mother, Claire, hadn't exactly reached a state of approval over our marriage, but by then she was resigned to it.

I think we'd been married for three days, when Val shook me awake at two o'clock in the morning.

'What do you want?' I asked sleepily.

'Are you awake?'

'Yes. You've just been shaking the bejeesus out of me. I'm awake.'

Val turned on the bedside light.

'I can't go,' she said. She swept a tangle of blonde curls away from her face. 'I'm sorry, I thought I could, but I can't leave everything I know and love and go to Australia with you. I'm sorry, but I can't.'

And with that off her chest she lay back down and turned off the light. A minute later a gentle snore told me she was asleep. I lay there, staring into the dark, and thinking... Oh shit! What now?

In the months leading up to the wedding, when I was out and about in Portland with her, and she would see somebody she knew, they would go through the hail-fellow-well-met stuff.

And when the acquaintance said, 'What's happening?' Val would say, 'Well, I'm getting married, and I'm moving to Australia.'

She loved the way their eyes popped when she said that. But then it turned into a reality: no longer an attention-grabbing line that caused people to gape. My panic was before we got married; Val's was after.

I talked to her sister Janet about it the next day. I liked Janet, she and Val were very close and she had her head screwed on straight. 'I'm not surprised, that sounds like Val,' was Janet's response. 'But don't worry, she'll go. She'll kick and scream and make your life miserable, but she'll get on the plane.'

I was happy about the get on the plane part, but I wasn't too pleased about the she'll make your life miserable bit.

***

When we packed to go to the airport, we had trouble getting everything we wanted to take into two suitcases. They were huge, but they weren't big enough to take all the wedding gifts and personal stuff we wanted to take. We called the airline, and somehow or other got the opinion that we were allowed two pieces of cabin baggage each. That solved some of the problem, but we still had to do a ruthless cull.

Departure Day. I didn't want to leave, but it was time to go. Bags were packed and stowed into trunks, family and hangers-on squeezed into eight cars that drove slowly to the airport like a funeral procession. Everyone's spirits were low. I was sad, but Val was infinitely sadder. She was leaving everything that she knew and loved. I know I was miserable, but whenever I looked at Val, and saw her big blue eyes filled with tears, I felt absolutely terrible. This person I loved so much was so sad and so scared.

But our fates were set: we were going. It was up to me to make it work.

When we got to the airport, we found that our information about two pieces of cabin baggage per passenger was wrong. We reorganised the bags, and put on two layers of clothes, and, where it was possible, three, and pushed and crammed and eventually got everything into the two big cases and two pieces of cabin baggage. We wouldn't be able to open the cabin baggage on the flight though. If we did the clothing would shoot out like pigeons released from a cage and land on other passengers.

All I can remember of the flight is that we felt like we were living a tragedy. I can remember one stage, it was dark, everyone was asleep, and I was sitting there amongst all these slumbering forms bawling my eyes out. I was going home, but I was going to miss my friends and the life I was leaving, and I was afraid of what lay ahead.

With the plane descending towards Sydney, we reorganised our cabin baggage. We carefully opened the two cabin bags, and took out two smaller bags. We took off all the extra clothes and repacked our cabin baggage into four bags.

As we were leaving the aircraft, one of the air crew looked goggle-eyed at our four pieces of carry-on and said, 'Wow. Congratulations. How did you manage that?'

I had been telling Val for a long time that my family would make a huge fuss over her when we arrived in Sydney. She got off the plane with her charm button set on high and looking like a million dollars – not an easy feat when you've been travelling for 20 hours and crying for a lot of that time. She was anticipating being the centre of attention when she met my family. We came out of customs, we looked around, but there was no family there to greet us.

Actually, they were there, they were just in the wrong place, watching the wrong exit out of customs. How typical of my family. When they found us, they descended on us in a pack, swallowed me in a melee of hugging, back-slapping and bonhomie. A minute later – Val says it was five – I looked back and saw my little lady in her pink dress, sitting on a suitcase looking lonely and forlorn. The pack returned, hugged and kissed her, gave her a bunch of flowers bigger than she was and swept her away with promises of champagne and good times.

***

We didn't have an ideal start to our life in Australia. We moved in with my brother Roger, in his house in one of Sydney's leafy and attractive northern suburbs. The house was an Edwardian style bungalow. Though it was a little run down I thought it was pretty cool. Val thought it was the pits. Her perspective was that we were a long way from home, neither of us had a job, we had two suitcases of belongings and $300, and we were living in a house that she thought was close to derelict.

The up side was that we were both well qualified and ambitious. Perusal of the Positions Vacant columns in the weekend papers gave us cause for optimism. Val got a job almost immediately. It took me three months.

That three months should have been enjoyable for me. I would see Val off on the train, and then I had the day to myself, in Sydney, in summer, with all those beaches and that beautiful weather. All I had to do was get dinner ready and meet Val at the station around 6 p.m. I should have enjoyed that time, but I didn't. Every day I bought the paper and scoured through the Positions Vacant. There were a lot of jobs, in teaching, in other areas where I thought I had a chance. But although I applied for many, the number of knock-backs was exactly equal to the number of applications. Most of the rejections were because I was over-qualified. Prospective employees didn't think a man with a Ph.D. was going to stay for long in the jobs I was applying for. They were right of course, but I didn't even get the opportunity to lie about how long I would stay.

I was persistent, but, as the days went by and rejection followed rejection, I was getting depressed. I kept thinking about Val at the airport in Oregon, how sad and scared she was but she was putting her faith and her future in my hands. No, I didn't enjoy that time, I just wanted to get a job. All I did was write applications, mope around the house, worry about letting Val down and wonder when my talents were going to be discovered.

My luck turned when I applied for a job as a deputy principal. I didn't get the job as a deputy principal, but the interviewers were impressed enough to offer me a job teaching science and maths. When I was offered the job I thought, science and maths? Me, teaching science and maths? Me, who ended up with a Ph.D. majoring in sport management because I'd avoided the science subjects? Me, who had passed maths only occasionally, very occasionally, in high school? But I needed a job, I took it, and, for the first time since we arrived in Sydney, we felt that we had something to celebrate.

I lasted in that job for three months, then I applied for a job teaching PE at another school. I stayed there for 18 months.

The best thing about that time of my life was that my life had become our life. I was happy, and I think my little blonde haired blue-eyed beauty was happy too. It sounds a little corny, but the two of us were becoming one, and I liked it.

The other positive thing was our digs. As soon as I got a job, we moved from the house in Wharoonga that Val thought was awful, to a small flat in Neutral Bay that was capital 'S' – Small. We stayed in Neutral Bay for a few months, and then moved to a flat in Kirribilli, which was very nice. The apartment itself was ordinary, but it was five floors up and had a view over the water to Circular Quay and the Opera House. We had what we called 'suicide windows' – floor to ceiling windows around three sides of the apartment. When you stood up close to them you got this feeling of vertigo like you were going to tumble through the glass to the street below – with glorious views of Sydney Harbour. We stayed there for six months, then I got a job lecturing in PE in Ballarat, at the Australian Catholic University.

Val was ropable about me taking that job. She didn't want to leave Sydney, and she was afraid that Ballarat was Hicksville. It was selfish of me, but I fought her on this issue because it was my opportunity to get into academia. We fought, she gave in, we moved to Ballarat.

We drove down to Ballarat. A couple of hours before we finally got there, we passed through Wombat State Forest. There are parts of that forest that are quite old, where the trees are tall and the undergrowth is heavy. I told Val that we were getting close to Ballarat. A minute later, I looked over at her and saw she had tears in her eyes.

I hate it when Val has the sads. 'What's the matter?' I asked.

'You're taking me to the boonies,' she said.

Ballarat is not, as Val first thought, the 'boonies'. It's a nice town, very historic. We lived there for a long time, and right to the end I would drive down some of its streets and think to myself it looks like a fairy town, with quaint little miners' cottages, big old trees lining the streets – very picturesque.

When we arrived in Ballarat, we quickly found that there was no employment available that would suit Val's career plans, so she took a job in Melbourne. For three-and-a-half years she drove to and from Melbourne every day. A 90-minute drive each way. Quite a noble effort.

Her first job didn't work out well, so she applied for a job as advertising manager for a sports magazine. She stayed there for three years, and the efforts of the owner to keep her were my first indication that, in the business world, my wife had talent.

***

We had been in Ballarat for two years when we bought an old school house, in Wattle Flat, 15 kilometres out of Ballarat. The shelter shed, and the outdoor girls' and boys' dunnies were still there. There were two old wool wagons in what would have been the playground, The place was as pretty as a postcard. God was in a really good mood when he created Wattle Flat. If a symphony was created for Wattle Flat, it would be called 'Harmony in Green'.

We moved into our new house in mid-winter. Winters in Ballarat are cold, and our new house had no insulation. The only heating was an open fireplace. In the kitchen, the ceiling was made up of loose three-ply slabs, with the tin roof showing through gaps in the plywood slabs; gaps wide enough to shoot the mice that inhabited the place in plague proportions, if we'd had a gun. We spent the winter being cold and killing mice. But it was our house.

I was like a pig in mud. We had a lovely old house in the country; I was working in academia, where the work was satisfying and the students were country kids – quiet, respectful, non-radical, with modest ambitions. Val quit her job in Melbourne and did consultancy work from home. Life was going well.

But before long I was again being hounded by the spirit of discontent.

Although I was enjoying my job at ACU, I was also finding it frustrating. It was a small institution, and I was, proverbially, hitting my head on the ceiling. Firstly, because I wasn't going to go anywhere in terms of career development, as health and physical education were not priority subjects. And secondly, I was teaching health and physical education when I wanted to teach sport management.

So, off I went again on a career search, while Val railed at me for upsetting the peaceful little applecart we'd built for ourselves in the old Wattle Flat schoolhouse.

I applied for a position teaching sport management at Southern Cross University in Lismore in northern New South Wales. I was offered it, accepted it, and our happy little Wattle Flat applecart was overturned.

I have this memory as clear as if it was yesterday. I was walking through the empty schoolhouse for what I thought was the last time. If ever a building spoke to a person, the old schoolhouse spoke to me. *I am part of you,* it said. *You are leaving a part of you behind.* The house was bare of furniture and trappings. As I walked towards the front door my shoes echoed on the yellow wood of the schoolroom floor. *You are leaving me,* said the house, *and I am empty.*

I closed the front door and locked it.

As we drove away, the grasses on either side of the road, prodded by the wind, waved goodbye.

Chapter 7: Pregnancy & Birth

In northern New South Wales, we started out in a rented house with views that stretched from the house at the top of a very steep ridge to the coastline and Byron Bay about ten kilometres away. It was a beautiful location.

We stayed there for six months, then we bought a house close to the beach. We moved in early August.

Our new house was on a canal, and 200 metres from the beach. It was a two-level kit home, with marble floors on the ground level, hardwood floors on the upper level, and fruit trees in the yard. A pretty house, in a pretty spot.

On the first night there, we lay in bed and listened to the rumble of the surf in the distance.

'Sounds like a freeway,' said Val.

Silly woman.

Our son Nathan was conceived soon after we moved in.

As soon as Val found she was pregnant she swore off alcohol and caffeine, she started walking every day, she took up yoga. She was as careful with the life growing inside her as any woman could have been. I have a photo of her when she was eight months pregnant – I should have more than one, but she wasn't very good about posing for photos when she was pregnant. In this photo Val looks so, so beautiful. Not just because pregnancy makes a woman glow, or more complete, or radiantly happy; she was beautiful because she was so fit.

I was, at last, where I wanted to be, teaching sport management at a regional university. The School of Human Movement at Southern Cross was very friendly, very tight. My first child was on the way. Life was good.

***

You'll know by now that I was a sports buff. I'd played, coached, watched, studied, read about, written about, and taught about sport my whole life. Now my wife was pregnant, and I knew my kid was going to be a champion. He was going to play for the Wallabies or she was going to win Wimbledon. He was going to coach Collingwood or she was going to win Olympic gold in several sports.

In my dreams, what was not going to happen was that my child would be born with severe cerebral palsy.

When that happened, all of the dreams died, and were replaced by black, black grief.

It was sad, and it was hard, but we got over it.

It is not the purpose of this story to describe the grief. This story is about overcoming it.

But even the story of getting over it is hard to write. Writing the story means re-living it. And some of it, still, when all the details are recalled, brings back the pain and grief that we've tried so hard to put behind us. On the up side though, writing means taking a helicopter view of where we started and where we are now, and that shows us what we've done, and what we've achieved, which is really pretty good.

Val and I stayed together for one thing, when about 80% of couples with severely disabled kids break up. We maintained our careers for another. Two professional careers in one family is difficult. With a disabled child… well, you can scarcely imagine.

Through it all, we believed that we'd had the most wonderful boy in the world.

If we'd had a choice, we would of course have preferred to have Nathan without his disability. But that wasn't an option we were offered. He was disabled. That was Nathan. And we'd rather have had Nathan with his disability than not at all. Dealing with his disability made life harder. But a hard life is not necessarily a bad life, just as an easy life is not necessarily a good one.

***

The various midwives who tended to Val throughout the birth showed a lot of concern that Nathan was suffering from a form of bradycardia. Every time Val had a contraction Nathan's heartbeat dropped very low, and it took a long time to come back to normal. It was the first clue we had that there were problems with his birth.

Nathan had a caesarean birth. This wasn't planned, and in hindsight, it was the second clue that something was wrong.

From what I've been told it is not standard practice for there to be a screen in the way during a caesarean birth, preventing a father from watching what's happening. There was one there in our case. It shielded me from seeing Val's lower half and what the doctors were doing while the operation was taking place. If we had known that this was not standard practice, the presence of the screen would have been the third clue.

Some hours after the birth, they gave me Nathan to hold. His head was cone-shaped, from the pressure that had been exerted on his skull before the decision to do a caesarean was made. The midwife assured me that he had a king-sized headache, but other than that he was fine.

Fine. Yeah!

I held my son. I looked down at this little package. It lay there, unmoving, totally unresponsive, looking off into the distance. That should have been the fourth clue.

I waited for the feelings of love, that I had been told parents experience when they first hold their offspring, to sweep over me.

Nothing.

Somewhere, deep, deep inside, I knew things weren't right, but I wasn't admitting it. And not admitting to myself that Nathan had problems was something that would go on for a long, long time.

I went home that night, and celebrated the birth of my son with some neighbours. 'A boy,' I crowed. 'We're going to call him Nathan. He's going to be a famous rugby player. Or maybe he'll be a golfer, or a track star. Who knows? He's my boy. He'll be able to do anything.'

My friends toasted me and my future champion son. The unspoken fears ebbed from my mind.

The next morning my life came crashing down. I walked into the hospital room and the paediatrician was standing at the end of the bed. Val had tears in her eyes. They were so blue, as big as saucers, and filled with alarm.

'We're a bit concerned,' said the paediatrician. 'There's a possibility that Bub has suffered some brain damage.'

He made it sound like it was an outside chance.

I leant forward, my fists on the bed. I think the pose may have looked a little aggressive, but I needed the support.

'A possibility?' I said. 'If you were a betting man, what odds would you give on that possibility?'

'I don't bet on the welfare of my patients,' said the paediatrician, which was his way of avoiding the issue.

Chapter 8: The Terror & Trauma of Learning That Your Newborn is Disabled

Let's be clear now, on what the issue was. When the paediatrician hedged on his concerns that Bub had suffered some brain damage, the issue was just that: did he, or did he not, have brain damage?

When we were told that there's a possibility that Bub has suffered some brain damage, we seized on the word *possibility*. The doctor said it was a possibility, he didn't say probability, and nobody – obstetricians, paediatricians, nursing staff, radiographers, neurologists or any of the countless other species that examined Nathan in those early days – would say that, yes, definitely, Nathan had brain damage.

If you're thinking that, as intelligent people, we should have been able to put the pieces together ourselves, you are right. But this was our child, our first child – our only one as it turned out – and the first child is something that we all dream of from the time we are old enough to understand the nuclear family concept. We didn't want to accept that our dream child was brain damaged, and we clung onto even the flimsiest possibilities that he wasn't. Whatever hopes were available to us, we dragged around us, draped ourselves in like refugees sheltering from a storm under thin pieces of gauze. We held to those flimsy possibilities as long as there was any reason to hope.

The first night after this awful news I stayed at my brother's place in Nimbin. Paul wasn't there; he was overseas. I missed him mightily that night. But a friend stayed with me. When I went to bed, Harold sat beside my bed in the dark, and listened to me talk and cry out my fears until I slept.

Val's brother Stephen came up from Melbourne. Once he arrived, he didn't know what to do or what to say, but he wanted to be there to support us.

Val told him what her fears were and Stephen said, 'It'll be alright, Val.'

He said it once too often and Val rounded on him in a rage. 'It won't be alright,' she spat. 'He's brain damaged. He'll never be normal. It won't be alright.' It was the only time in the first few weeks that those words were spoken out loud.

'I don't know what else to say,' said Steve.

He took me to play golf. He wanted to help, and didn't know what else to do. I got half way through the front nine and gave up. It's hard to concentrate on a golf ball when you think your life is in ruins.

Up until the day Stephen arrived, I'd stayed most nights in the hospital with Val and Nathan. But Stephen wasn't able to stay there, so I drove him to our place in Golden Beach. Under normal circumstances I would have played the proud home-owner, showing off my fruit trees, the beautiful beach, the canal that was my backyard swimming pool. But circumstances were not normal, and showing off of any kind was impossible.

Nathan was five days old by this time, and the nights since his birth had been nights of broken sleep, black grief, abject misery, and forlorn, desperate hopes. That night, as I lay in bed, still awake at 2 a.m., I did my best to be brave. And, more than anything else, I was trying to convince myself that this wasn't going to get me down. I was going to get through it, and I was going to take Val and my boy with me.

And maybe it would all be a false alarm.

The next day, when I was in the hospital room by myself – they had given us a private room, and, as often as we were falling apart, we needed it – I picked up my tiny, broken child. I put him inside my shirt and against my chest. I promised him that I would always, always look after him.

I shouldn't have had to do that, but at this point I still wasn't feeling fatherly waves of love washing through me. Maybe the stress and the grief were so dominant they hid all the other feelings. I don't know why, but I had to do something to reassure myself that, even if the worst came to the worst, even if my son had suffered brain damage, I would fulfil my obligations as a father.

My little brother Roger – he's 15 cm taller than me, but he's still my *little* brother – drove up from Sydney. It was an 18-hour drive. He came by himself. He got out of the car in front of our house and I went out to meet him. He put his arms around me. I leaned against him and cried like I'd never stop.

Val's sister Cathy came out from the Vermont. She came because she wanted to support her sister. But once she arrived, there wasn't much she could do.

***

There was a brief time, about two weeks after the birth, when we managed to convince ourselves that all the signals had been wrong, that we'd had a nasty scare but there was nothing wrong with Nathan after all. This came after several sources gave us evidence that allowed us to fool ourselves that our fears were unfounded.

First, we met with some early intervention specialists in Lismore. They told us that it was very naughty of the doctors to tell us that Nathan had brain damage, because it was so early in his development that it was impossible to tell. We seized on those words like passengers from the Titanic would have seized onto tiny pieces of driftwood that couldn't possibly keep them afloat.

Second, Nathan had a cat-scan done at the hospital. It showed that the brain activity in the outer cortex was virtually non-existent. That should have been enough to tell us again what we didn't want to know, but the technician, trying to mask the bad news, assured us that at the age of 15 days it was hard to put much faith in what a cat-scan showed. Again, we hung onto those words as though life itself depended on them. We used them as clubs, to beat away the plethora of other indicators that told us what was clear to more objective minds.

Third, the paediatrician organised for an MRI to be done on Nathan. When he looked at the results, he said there were some very significant anomalies. But then he turned his attention to Nathan and he said, 'But we treat the child, not the brain-scans.'

64

Incredibly, that statement again gave us hope. It was like he was dismissing the scans as misleading or unimportant. And when I talked to one of my colleagues at work, and told him about the MRI results, he told me of a child he knew that was absolutely normal, who had an MRI done and was told by the experts that he would never walk or talk in his life. With this news, and the paediatrician's words, we managed to convince ourselves that the MRI, like the cat scans and the naughty words from the doctors, didn't mean anything.

Fourth and finally, we looked up some research articles on cerebral palsy, and in one of them we read that the condition of a CP sufferer may never be noticed by the rest of the population. The article explained that the parts of the brain that are damaged may not be the motor controlling parts, so movement wouldn't be affected. We grasped at that possibility, and told ourselves that, if Nathan did have CP, it would be minor enough for our boy to live a normal life.

Our self-delusion did not last long. It came to an end when we were sent to Brisbane to talk to an infant neurology specialist. He welcomed us, offered us tea or coffee and made small talk while he went through Nathan's data. He read the paediatrician's report, looked at the cat-scans, looked at the brain-scans. Then he picked Nathan up and went through a gentle tossing-type action as though weighing him in his hand.

His next statement crashed into us like head punches.

'It's black and white,' he said. 'This boy has cerebral palsy.'

There was a long, long silence. When I was able to talk, I asked, 'How bad?'

'Moderate severity,' he said.

With hindsight I can say that I wish he'd been right, because, as it turned out, Nathan's CP put him in the 95th percentile of severity. But, even with a prediction of moderate CP, the words were as terrifying as a prison sentence.

We left the neurologist's office believing that our lives were shattered. Val held the crib with this tiny, brain damaged little being in it. Tears were pouring down her face.

'What are we going to do?' she asked. The despair in her voice was as naked as a blade.

I didn't reply. I couldn't. I didn't know what we were going to do.

In the two-hour drive back to Golden Beach, not a word was spoken.

Over the next few weeks, all we could do was take one day at a time. We woke each morning to a nightmare. It stayed with us all day, and was still there with us when we went to bed. The normal routine for parents with a newborn child is one of broken sleep, peaks of joy brought about by that first smile, by the baby cooing, by congratulations from friends as the new-borne is shown off. All we got was the broken sleep. We got no smiles, no baby cooing. We got bad dreams, and commiserations from friends instead of congratulations.

Many parents start making long term plans for their children when they're just a few months old. For us, long term was too frightening to contemplate.

When Nathan was about a month old, I got a call from the head of the School of Human Movement at Federation University. He called to tell me that there was a job going in sport management in his school. 'And by the way,' he added, 'your old house is on the market.'

The old schoolhouse. Wattle Flat. Happy days in a past life that we could escape back to.

It's hard to remember exactly what our thought processes were when I was offered that job, but it came at a time when we were badly messed up. Our memories of Wattle Flat were of a lovely old house, a tight friendship circle and a town we knew well. I still wonder if we would have gone back if we hadn't suffered the tragedy we'd just suffered. At the time, we saw it as an escape from our nightmare.

Before we left Golden Beach, Val called the hospital in Lismore. 'I want copies of all of the records relating to Nathan's birth,' she told the administrator.

'Why do you want them?' the woman asked. 'Do you intend to sue?'

'Why? Do you think we should?' asked Val, with her tongue planted firmly in her cheek.

'Umm... why... err... no,' said the woman. 'I was just curious as to why you would want them.'

Val wanted the records because they might provide clues about Nathan's disability, but she was angry at the hospital and all who worked, resided or inhabited therein, so she wasn't going to let them off the hook too easily.

'Well, thank you for the suggestion of a law suit,' she said. 'It could be one of the reasons that I might need the files in the future. Please send them to me as soon as possible.'

When we arrived back at Wattle Flat, we put the furniture back as it used to be, hung the pictures back in the same places. It was late June. Winter sunlight streamed in through the window, turning the old school room into shades of shadow and gold. You are home said the house. I will care for you.

On the surface nothing had changed. But now we had this little bundle of life. It was defective. It was our job to love it.

We were back home, but very, very unhappy.

Chapter 9: Not Knowing

When I read back over what I've said in the preceding chapter it sounds as though I didn't love my newborn kid. It's hard to remember exactly what my feelings were in those months after his birth, but I probably didn't. I think that, for a while, with all the problems he had, and as scary as his problems were, fear outweighed love.

I cared for him, and I cared about him. Maybe I cared because I thought I had to care. Society, logic, basic human values, all told me that it was my role to care.

Did I love him then? I don't think so.

Do I love him now? You betcha!

The worst thing about those early days though, wasn't not knowing if I loved Nathan, it was not knowing how severe his disability would be. Not knowing if he would walk, talk, see, hear, go to school, go out on a date, have anything approaching a normal life.

Actually, we totally believed he would do all of those things. We just wanted to know how well.

In the first few months of Nathan's life, we saw so many specialists who told us so many different things, that we started to lose track of who said what. We looked into different ways of caring for a CP kid, and found so much conflicting information that we didn't know who or what to believe. Yet, at the end of each week, at the end of each month, at the end of each year, for the first four of five years, we still didn't know how bad Nathan's disability would be.

And not knowing was awful.

We believed that, with help, Nathan would walk, so we spent a couple of years taking him to Melbourne once a week for Conductive Education therapy. Val one week, me the next, which was an interruption to both our professional lives. We wrote up what we did in these sessions, and took the exercises home with us as homework to do each night. We would go through the notes together, show what was done, do it all again. After doing this for a year a Conductive Education program started up in Ballarat. Twice a week, 3.30-4.30 p.m., we put Nathan through a program that stretched his body and, we hoped, his intellect. We worked, watched, and waited for a miracle that never came.

The Conductive Education therapists told us about Point Percussion therapy. As an addendum to Conductive Education, they said. So once a month, on a Saturday morning, we drove to Melbourne to take Nathan to Point Percussion therapy.

The Point Percussion sessions were in south Melbourne, which wasn't too bad, but after a year the therapist moved her practice out to Mitcham and that made the drive almost twice as long. The therapist realized how difficult it was, and referred us to a Chinese Point Percussion practitioner who lived a lot closer. His methods combined Chinese massage techniques with Point Percussion therapy, with some extraordinary results, she said.

This specialist's name was Dr. Po. He ran a series of workshops that varied from one day to a full week. The first workshop we enrolled Nathan in was a full week. I took the week off work, booked into a motel, and prepared myself for that miracle.

I cannot remember everything we did in that week, but I do remember being told by the doctor to dig the tips of my fingernails into Nathan's cuticles to stimulate the nerve receptors. Have you ever tried doing that? To yourself or to anyone else? It hurts like bloody hell. I was told to squeeze hard with my fingernails, into every one of Nathan's cuticles. Every time I did it, he jumped like he'd been given an electric shock. That's how desperate we were. My poor little kid. And, of course, there was no miracle.

We had hearing tests done on Nathan, and got the only good news we'd had until that time. His hearing was unaffected by his cerebral palsy.

That was a good day.

We went to see an eye specialist and were told that Nathan was, in all practical terms, blind. 'He has eyesight,' said the specialist, 'but at the point where the optic nerve links into the brain, the damage is so bad that Nathan cannot interpret the signals that are coming from eye to brain. He's suffering what is called Cortical Visual Impairment.'

That was a bad day.

To deal with his CVI, we took Nathan to therapy sessions at the Royal Victorian Institute for the Blind. Those sessions were in Burwood, in Melbourne's eastern suburbs – a three-hour drive from Ballarat. We did that drive, Val one week, me the next, once a week for two years, until we were recommended to a specialist with a big reputation, who was on secondment at the Melbourne Eye and Ear Hospital.

I think the guy's name was Hector. Hector asked me to tell him about Nathan's eyesight.

'He's got Cortical Visual Impairment,' I said, rolling the words off my tongue like an expert. 'It's severe enough that he is, in effect, blind.'

Hector looked into Nathan's eyes with a weird instrument. He waved a bright red streamer around in front of him like a witch doctor performing a voodoo ritual. He sat back and studied Nathan for a moment.

'How do you know he's suffering from Cortical Visual Impairment?' he asked.

The simplest answer would have been to quote the eye specialists from Ballarat and the RVIB who had told us about this affliction. But I wanted to sound smarter than that so I echoed the words we had been told and said, 'He avoids looking at things because he's not able to interpret them.'

'If he avoids looking at them, he's got to be able to see them,' said Hector with stunning logic. 'And if he can see them, he's not blind, is he?'

I had no answer for that. I think Nathan was six years old, and we'd been taking him to the RVIB since he was four. It seemed like this guy was about to tell me that those trips to Melbourne, once a week for two years, were a waste of time. My scepticism must have shown on my face.

'You want me to prove that he can see?' asked Hector.

My head went up and down like a jack hammer.

Hector held an M&M candy in front of Nathan's face, about 60 centimetres away, and took it through this weird circling motion as he moved it towards him. When the piece of candy approached Nathan's face, he opened his mouth to receive it.

Hector glanced over at me. He saw my mouth was hanging open and I'm sure he knew it wasn't because I wanted an M&M. 'Want me to do it again?' he asked, 'just to prove it wasn't a fluke?'

I nodded, harder this time. Hector took another M&M through the same circling pattern, and Nathan's mouth opened to receive it.

'He's got lots of vision,' said Hector – I thought this was an odd way to put it, I'd heard of people having good or bad vision, but I'd never heard of them having a lot of vision – 'but he doesn't know how to use it. He needs to be taught, encouraged or bullied into seeing what's in front of him.'

Having a kid like Nathan is like riding on the Big Dipper at Luna Park: you swing up, you swing down, you whizz around in great big heart-lurching circles. The drive home was an upswing. When I told Val what Hector had said she laughed, cried, and laughed again. Three years after we'd found that Nathan could hear we celebrated our second piece of good news.

***

With every one of the techniques and therapies that we tried, we hoped for signs that Nathan would be able to walk and talk. I had this fantasy about going to a clinic in Hungary that was the birthplace of Conductive Education. In my dream, Nathan and I would come home from the Hungarian clinic, Val would meet us at the airport, and Nathan would walk out of the customs gate and into her tearful and overjoyed embrace. I'm sure Val had similar dreams, and we pursued every lead and every possibility and went to ridiculous extremes in trying to realise them. We searched. We worked. We watched. We waited. And we hoped.

And hoped.

And hoped.

What we were hoping for changed through the years.

First, we hoped our son would not be disabled. Then, after accepting that he was going to be disabled we hoped that the disability wouldn't be too bad, though neither of us knew what too bad was. Through this time, at least once a week one of us would say, 'If only we knew what was coming.'

Weeks turned into months. Months turned into years. Specialists would tell us things that boosted our hopes, another would tell us something else. We still didn't know what was coming, we just kept hoping.

A few months after birth, Nathan developed epilepsy. We were told by a specialist that it might pass as his brain matured. So that's what we hoped, or maybe we believed that, around the time that he spoke his first words or took his first steps, he would stop fitting. But somewhere in those first few years, it became clear that he was going to suffer badly from this affliction. I don't know when we stopped hoping for that miracle.

One small blessing was that he didn't suffer full-blown grand mal seizures. But, in his infancy, he had these ticky little fits, short little things that wouldn't leave him alone. Each one would last a fraction of a second, as short as a blink, but he had thousands every day.

Short little fits. A fraction of a second. Doesn't sound too bad, does it?

Nathan was also non-verbal. He wasn't able to relay complex information, like how did that fit make you feel Nathan? So, we weren't able to interpret from his non-verbal cues how these little fits affected him. But I think it went like this:

My dad... *blink*. Where was I?

Oh yeah, my dad wants to... *blink*. Where was I?

Oh yeah, my dad wants to give me some... *blink*. Where was I?

Oh yeah, my dad wants to give me some food... *blink*. Where was I?

Oh yeah, my dad wants to give me some food so I need to open... *blink*. Where was I?

And so on, through every waking moment.

Through early childhood, he would intersperse these ticky

little fits with larger ones that lasted up to 20 seconds. These larger fits fell into two categories.

First, there were the two-to-five-second fits, which Nathan really seemed to enjoy. As soon as they are finished, he'd break out into a huge grin. Experts have told us that an epilepsy sufferer can see bright colours when they fit, or hear a ringing in the ears, or experience something akin to an orgasm. I hoped that Nathan's short category fits were like an orgasm. He sure seemed to enjoy them.

The second category were the fits that were longer than five seconds. They'd knock him around a fair bit. He'd moan, grimace, go rigid all over and his limbs would jerk spasmodically. After they finished, he usually went to sleep. I hated these fits. I especially hated the grimaces. I had been assured that he wasn't in pain, but it looked like he was.

Apparently, he had a type of epilepsy called Lennox Gastaut Syndrome, and it was one of the worst kinds of epilepsy. According the 'syndromespedia.com' website, the complications associated with Lennox Gastaut Syndrome are:
• Injuries from seizure
• Renal, cardiac, or metabolic complications resulting from a Ketogenic diet (a diet that helps suppress epileptic seizures)
• Disconnection syndrome resulting from corpus callosotomy surgical procedure (surgery for the treatment of seizures)
• Language disorders brought about by the corpus callosotomy procedure
• Motor dysfunction as a result of the corpus callosotomy procedure
• Neurophysical impairment associated with the corpus callosotomy procedure
• Mental retardation as time progresses
• Death

Forget the first seven; look at the last one. When we dug a little further, we found that a significant percentage of Lennox Gastaut sufferers died at an early age, in their sleep. For years, after finding that out, we would go into Nathan's room in the mornings, almost too afraid to look.

We tried just about every epilepsy drug on the market except for steroids. As an epilepsy drug, steroids have bad side effects. For Nathan, steroids would have been a drug of last resort. Fortunately, we never had to use them.

We did have some early success in controlling his epilepsy. He was taking three different drugs, and the fits, for a while, were fully controlled. We were told that the fitting was likely to return, but that there was an outside chance that his epilepsy may pass as his brain matures. Put yourself in our shoes: you're chasing rainbows, waiting for a miracle and hoping, hoping, hoping.

And then your child stops fitting.

Of course, you believe what you want to believe, that the epilepsy is passing as your child's brain matures.

What do you do, then? You wean him off the drugs, because he doesn't need them anymore.

I remember when we gave Nathan what we thought was his last dose of epilepsy drugs and ceremonially dropped the unused drugs into the rubbish bin. We were on holiday in Apollo Bay at the time, and it was a cause for celebration.

But, by the time we got home a couple of days later, the fits had started again. We hoped it would be temporary. The paediatrician had told us that they might re-surface briefly when Nathan was weaned off the drugs, but they could quickly fade. By mid-week fading was the last thing they were doing, and by the end of the week they were again hitting him at a rate of thousands per day. We were told to count them across a 15-minute period, and use that as a basis for calculating how many he had in a day. In 15 minutes, he had 200. You figure it out.

We went back to the regime of three different epilepsy drugs, but for quite some time they had little effect. We used to joke that we should look into a way to hook Nathan up to a generator. He'd produce enough electricity to power our house. The joking stopped when we went to see a neurologist in Melbourne, and received this sobering news: 'Nathan's lifespan is likely to be much shorter than yours. His longevity depends largely on whether or not we can control his fitting.'

At that time his fitting was wildly out of control.

That meeting was one of the times when our hopes for a miracle disappeared, and cold reality hit us like a bucket of iced water.

The fitting remained a significant problem for several years, until Nathan copped a lucky break when he underwent hip surgery at the Royal Children's Hospital. Something was amiss after the operation and he was in immense pain. He was given doses of Valium that were big enough to knock out a horse. Valium works on the brain, and while Nathan was on the Valium he didn't fit. We kept the doses up for several days, and then gradually eased him off the drug, all the while waiting for and dreading the reappearance of the fits. But they didn't show. He didn't stop fitting altogether, we had to continue on with the three other medications, but he was fitting a lot less and the short ticky fits – tonic-clonic is the proper name for the little bastards – had disappeared altogether. It was a cause for a major celebration.

***

Through infancy and into early childhood Nathan looked like any little kid. At the time, this was important, because it allowed me to go out in public with him and not feel the shame of having a disabled kid.

Shame?

Why?

Dunno, but it was there.

Although he didn't look disabled, at three, four, five, he didn't look like a kid of that age. He looked much younger. And, if you observed him closely, you'd notice that his head was small.

The small head was one of the first things the specialists all noticed. We'd take Nathan into their rooms, they'd introduce themselves, they'd turn their attention to Nathan and their eyes would widen. Then they'd reach for a tape measure to measure the circumference of his head.

In those years, I used to think about how much like any other normal little boy he looked. I wondered how long it would be before others no longer saw him as normal.

When he was three, we were on a shopping trip in Melbourne. Shopping trips: my wife loves them; I hate them. On this one, as we entered yet another women's clothing store, a salesgirl rushed up to Nathan and went all gooey over him. She commandeered his stroller and took charge of him for the time that we were in her store. She told us how much he looked like a tiny adult rather than a baby. I was appreciative, maybe a little jealous, of the attention my boy was getting from this gorgeous chick, but I wondered how she would react if she knew that Nathan was a cerebral palsy child who suffered from severe epilepsy. I didn't tell her about these things, but I wondered how long it would be before people's reaction changed from, oh what a cute baby, to, oh look at that poor child.

At the time of this incident, I was still clinging to the hope that Nathan's CP would be mild enough for him to live a normal life, so I dreaded the possibility of him looking disabled. But when that became the reality, like everything else about having a disabled kid in a wheelchair, I got used to it.

Part 3: How We Got There

Chapter 10: Adjustment

When I arrived at Federation University, and the head of my department heard the news about my son, he was sympathetic. He told me that if I needed to leave work at any time to deal with issues related to Nathan, he would understand. In fact, the whole department accepted that I had a unique problem and that my kid came first. When I had to go to Melbourne for Conductive Education, my lectures were rostered so I had Thursday afternoons free. When I had to go to the RVIB, the whole day was kept lecture-free. When Nathan had an emergency – and he had many over the years – they covered for me, whether I needed to spend days or weeks away from work.

Being career oriented and caring for Nathan fitted together okay. We have our colleagues at Federation University to thank for making it that way. We will forever be indebted to them.

Nathan was a few months old when I finally told some of my colleagues about him. It was hard, *very* hard, for a macho guy who was fit, into sport and manly things, so I didn't tell many of them. I just let the news kind of filter out. The result of that was that some of them weren't sure that they were supposed to know, so they carefully avoided the subject of my child's health and wellbeing.

I asked myself over and over why the subject of Nathan's disability was, for some years, a touchy subject, and it came down to two things. First, it had something to do with grief. Grief is very personal. I wanted to be left alone with my grief. Second, there was an element of shame and guilt that my son wouldn't be able to do what 'normal' people do.

Shame is a sense of being inadequate or defective; guilt is a wish to undo what has been done. These emotions are, apparently, common in grieving people and essential to their recovery. But I think the feelings of shame and guilt were exacerbated by where I worked, at the School of Human Movement at Federation

University. Colleagues and students were all into health, fitness, sport. They spent their time running, swimming, in the weights room, out on the sports field, studying. My kid was not going to do what the people I worked with did. In my world of academic and sporting competition, I felt that I hadn't measured up, that I was a failure.

***

I'll say it again. Carrying two careers in one family is difficult. Carrying two careers in a family with a severely disabled kid is really, really difficult. We managed it, on the back of support from our colleagues, and through careful and consistent consideration of the demands of each other's careers.

From the outset, we agreed that our first consideration was Nathan. Then everything else pretty much fell into place behind that.

When we first got married, we agreed that whoever's career was doing best would get first consideration on where we went, where we lived, what we did. A great agreement for me, I thought. I had a Ph.D., a clearly defined career path. Though Val had two undergraduate degrees, one in marketing and one in communications, she had no clear career path. She would never match it with me career-wise, right?

Yeah, right!

When we arrived in Australia Val had gotten a job with a small publishing company. Her boss loved her, and when we moved to Victoria, she was sorry to see her go. Val's first job in Melbourne had been with a printing company, but she didn't stay there long because she didn't like to work in chaos. Her next job was with another publishing company, and they, again, loved her. The company owner was so keen to keep her that, two years later, when she said she was quitting because it was too expensive for her to drive every day from Ballarat to Melbourne, he bought Val's car, gave her the use of it and paid her a weekly petrol allowance to cover the travel costs. When she was finally tired of driving to Melbourne every day, her boss gave her a job as a work-from-home consultant, which she did until we moved north.

When we moved from Lismore, where Nathan was born, back to Ballarat, Val didn't have a job. She was a mum, and she had a kid that was going to require lots and lots of attention. We both believed that a career was going to be of secondary importance to her, for a few years anyway. But, as a sage once said, "Life is what happens to you while you're planning for the future". And while we were planning how we were going to care for Nathan, as an infant, a child, an adolescent, Val's needs emerged.

Val is a challenge-oriented person, and while the challenge of looking after Nathan was a big one, it wasn't big enough for Val. She needed the challenges that only a career could provide. Since Nathan's birth she has had three jobs worthy of mention. The first one was as General Manager at a locally owned company. The second was at Federation University.

In 1997, she started at the University as the Manager of Student Recruitment. In her time there, she had a series of promotions, and ended up as the Director of Student Services, responsible for a 100 staff, spread across six campuses, with a salary that was nearly twice the size of mine.

You remember that agreement? That whoever's career was doing best would get first consideration on where we went, where we lived, what we did? I was going to be top dog for the length of our working lives.

Yeah, right!

She went by me so fast she was out of hailing distance before I knew it. Having two careers and a disabled kid in one family is difficult, but it didn't slow Val down at all. She is a very capable career woman – and occasionally just a little bit difficult to live with – but my favourite way of describing her relates to her qualities as a mother: if God had written a recipe for the ideal mum for Nathan, he would have come up with a Val. She is the ultimate organiser and planner, and a tireless advocate for her boy. A disabled kid needs a parent like that.

I said that Val has had three jobs worthy of mention. The third one is the job she took when we left Ballarat, as Executive Director of Marketing and Admissions at a Gold Coast university. Whatta gal!

***

I wish I could be a little clearer in explaining our adjustment to Nathan's disability in the early years of his life. I know we did adjust, because we loved Nathan like crazy and were not fazed by his disability. But it was a long, slow and often painful journey.

To get where we ended up, we went through four phases. Do not, on any of these phases except the first one, expect to be told how long each one lasted, because we don't know.

The first phase was grief and denial. In those early days we thought we'd never get past the grieving, but gradually we learnt that you can't grieve forever – you have to accept what is and move on. Still, it took us a long time to move on.

That we would grieve is not surprising, we had lost the dream of a perfect child. That we would deny Nathan's disability is slightly more complex.

We did though, for a time after he was born, deny what was undeniable, and it was an amazing piece of self-delusion. When you're facing something that's terrifying, you can come up with the most elaborate ways of hiding from the truth. But I think there was some value in this; I think we hid from the truth just long enough to subconsciously allow ourselves to adjust to it. Adjustment started after we saw the neurologist in Brisbane and the truth was pretty much stripped bare. The final revelation came when Nathan was four months old, when Val flew from Lismore to Sydney on her way to Ballarat.

She left Lismore earlier than I did so she could see a specialist in Sydney. She took our five-year-old nephew Geordie with her. The specialist told Val that there was no doubt that Nathan would have a significant disability. She pointed at Geordie and said, 'There is simply no chance that he will be like this little boy here.'

When Val called me that evening, and told me of the specialist's words, my heart sunk down into my boots and kept on going. So now, with indisputable evidence, we knew we had to stop hiding from the truth. We had a child with a disability.

End of the denial part of phase one. The grieving part went on for a long time, overlapping with phase two.

Phase two was when we accepted that Nathan had a disability but we hoped it wouldn't be too bad. We clung to that hope for some years. I can remember when Nathan was three, thinking, that by the time he was five, he would have taken some steps, and that, by the time he was seven, he would be able, maybe with help, to walk out to the car. This hope was aided by one of my colleagues. Brad was a motor learning lecturer, and the statement that he made that gave Val and me so much hope was that the mileposts for Nathan would be further part. That was all. To our grasping-at-straws brains, the mileposts being further apart inferred that he would still reach them, it would just take him a bit longer.

It took us many years to stop hoping that Nathan would reach those developmental mileposts. An example of what we went through in this stage was when Nathan was three and we were seeing a point percussion therapist. After we'd been travelling to Melbourne to see her for some months, we asked her if Nathan would walk one day. She lifted Nathan up by the arms, and kind of bounced him gently up and down so his feet were hitting the massage table. Nathan reacted by setting his little legs into a frantic walking action.

'Oh yes,' she said with a laugh, 'he'll walk someday. He may find it difficult, but he'll walk.'

The difference in one's life – between a child that can walk and one that can't – is as huge as an ocean. As we drove home, we were almost weeping with joy. We got drunk that night on the euphoria of the therapist's prediction.

But Nathan never managed to do any kind of walking action again.

As the years went by, we held on to the hope that Nathan's disability wouldn't be too bad, and we held on with an iron grip. But there is a difference between hope and delusion, and eventually we had to let go of that hope.

Phase three was when we removed the rose-coloured lens and accepted the reality of our son's disability. Dealing with this phase was, again, a long, slow and often painful process. It involved ridding ourselves of the last vestiges of grief – not the regret though, we will always have the regret – and accepting the total reality of Nathan's disability. This reality had multiple parts. Let me explain some of them.

The reality was that Nathan had an epilepsy problem. However, we did not see him as an epileptic, because a specialist developed a drug regime that kept his fitting under control. He still had some fits, and every now and then they became too persistent and we had to tinker with his drug regime. When we were in phase two, we believed the epilepsy was something he would grow out of. Oddly enough, we didn't accept that it was a permanent part of his life until we were able to control it.

Another reality was that he lived in permanent danger from chest infections. He had only one fully functioning lung, and we had been told that it was likely that it would be a chest infection that ended his life. We lived in dread of chest infections. Even a common cold was scary.

And another reality was that he was non-verbal. For the most part this was a minor disadvantage because we could still communicate with him at a yes-no level. But when something was going wrong, and he could not tell us what it was, small problems became big ones.

Imagine this little dilemma: he's put in his wheelchair just slightly askew, so most of his weight is on one buttock. He can't shift himself around to even things up, and he can't tell us that he's getting stiff and sore in that one cheek.

So, he'd have to live with that problem all day. He did, however, know how to communicate with someone who knew him well and was paying attention. If he cried it was because he was hurting. He never, ever, cried just to get attention. If he was asked a yes-no question, he looked left for yes and right for no, or he smiled such a happy, heart-warming smile there was no doubt he was saying yes. If he yelled for us in the middle of the night, we knew there was a problem.

Sometimes, though, he got a laughing fit, and, for some odd reason, these often happened late at night. We woke when we heard what sounded like yelling, and we ran into his room to see what was wrong, only to find he was laughing his deeply contagious belly laugh for no reason that we could figure out.

The reality was that he was in the 95th percentile of disability. If Nathan was lying by the seashore, and the tide was coming in, and he had to lift his head just a few centimetres off the sand to keep his head above water, he couldn't have done it. Acknowledging that that was to be his lot in life was very, very hard.

The reality was that Nathan would most probably die before us. Predictions about Nathan's life expectancy varied from 15 to 40 years. We'd already made it past 15 and were planning on kicking the shit out of the 40, but that didn't change the likelihood of him going before us.

Like any parent who has to think about their offspring dying before they do, the thought of losing Nathan scared the bejesus out of us. However, it was more than just losing someone we love. Without Nathan, we would be less somehow – not as important. People looked at Nathan and saw someone with high needs. Then they looked at us and saw the people who were taking care of Nathan's needs. It made us feel... I don't know, significant, maybe.

We knew then that Nathan was never going to walk a single step, lift a spoon to his mouth, date a girl, swim a lap or tell his mom and dad that he loved them. So, he was disabled: we finally could say it with a shrug. It added some hardship to our lives, but what is life without hardship? Once we were able to tell ourselves these things, we'd moved into the fourth and final phase. We both wish we had started with this phase, but I guess we had to get the grieving, hoping and adjusting out of the way first.

The final phase of adjusting to our son's disability was Let's Get On With It. In this, there was no grief. Instead, we concentrated on what Nathan could do, not by grieving over what he couldn't. To reach this phase we had to let go of hoping he would achieve the developmental mileposts we earlier hoped he would reach. We had to accept what we had. Once we achieved that, we were able to build Nathan's repertoire of meaningful experiences.

It should be understood though, that we only reached this stage because we got a lot of help from Nathan. That is not a rosy interpretation, it is the indisputable truth. He helped us to understand that what he can't do only looks frightening if you ignore what he can do. He could make the people around him smile, he could make them laugh, and he had shown us a number of times that, above all else, he was a fighter. He wanted to live, and from that it automatically follows that he wanted to make the best of his life.

It should also be said that we reached the final phase of acceptance with significant help from a number of Nathan's carers. The carers were a huge part of his life. We had possibly a hundred of them over the years. Some of them we wouldn't recognize now if we saw them; they only stayed long enough to decide that Nathan was in the too-hard-basket, or they turned out to be a little less than 100% reliable and we had to let them go. Others stayed and made an impact. A very small number have become our friends.

Close to retirement, a straight speaking and 100% reliable individual who was worth listening to, Jane was one of them. She has been there to help us through at the worst of times, and to celebrate at the best.

Kellie was another. A student nurse, she looked after Nathan when he was six, seven and eight. It was a crucial time for us: it was when we were giving up on those developmental mileposts and when we were just starting to look, instead, at what Nathan could do. Kellie helped us through the peaks and troughs of that time.

She came home late with Nathan one afternoon. I had been worrying, so I gave her a serve. Unperturbed by my angst she said, 'We went to buy Nathan a blow-up beach chair. He told me he wanted one, but he wouldn't tell me if he wanted a green or a red one, so we had to stay there until he told me.'

I was sceptical. 'How did you know he wanted a beach chair?'

'You're going to the beach for a holiday soon. I told him about blow-up beach chairs and he said he wanted one.'

'Kel, he can't talk. How did he tell you he wanted one?'

She looked at me with contempt. 'He's your son, and you

don't know how to listen to him other than listening to his voice? When I asked if he wanted one, he told me with his face that he did. It just took him a long time to tell me which colour.'

We had been told by various experts of different ways of communicating, but methods like ComPic, computer programs and other things undoubtedly worked for other kids but not for a severely disabled kid like Nathan. Kellie taught us to watch Nathan's face closely and interpret what he wanted to say from his expression and the movements of his head. There was not the least doubt in her mind that he listened, and that he processed what he heard. The skill of watching Nathan – intently and patiently – was one we were still working on, and we were getting better at it. You can tell lots from a twist of the head, a quirk of the eyebrows, a frown, a smile. Like Kellie said, he could tell us what he was thinking, it just took him a while.

There was another time, when Nathan was still taking his food orally, when Kellie announced, 'I think I've taught Nathan to chew gum.'

'It's not really a skill that he needs, Kel,' I replied.

She gave me that look again. 'It's a good way for him to practice chewing,' she said. And, indeed, she had taught him to chew gum, but Val kyboshed it. She was afraid of Nathan inhaling a wad of gum into his lungs. What it showed us though was that, like Kellie, we should have more faith in what Nathan could do.

Nathan, of course, did not set out to help us get over worrying about his disability, or to encourage us to get on with our lives. But make no mistake, he helped us with both of those things. While we were worrying about how to deal with his immobility, his lungs, epilepsy, vision problems, learning difficulties, speech impediments, poor communications and limited life prospects, it gradually dawned on us that Nathan was a happy little bloke. He wasn't worrying about what he couldn't do, he was enjoying his life as it unfolded.

When we saw that, we started paying more attention to what he had to teach us.

A significant lesson came when, at seven years, he showed us how well he could tune in to what's going on around him. We were Christmas shopping. You know what shopping malls are like at Christmas: a buzzing, hurrying, happy mass of humanity. When we entered the mall, Nathan's head came up, his eyes opened wide, and he smiled. He stayed alert and smiling for the three hours that we were there. He couldn't run into a store and buy something, he couldn't tell us what he wanted us to buy, he had no use for 99% of what was on sale, and what he did have a use for wasn't exciting anyway. But he was happy to be there, happy to be part of that happy atmosphere.

Reinforcement of that lesson came when Nathan was eight. We took him to a football game at the MCG: one of the blockbusters, a sell-out. When we entered the stadium, it was humming like a beehive. The reaction from Nathan was the same as when we went shopping. His head came up, his eyes opened wide, he smiled. And he stayed that way throughout the game. The best thing was, every time a goal was scored and the crowd roared its approval, it was like Nathan thought they were cheering for him. He cracked up every time. How much of the game he understood I don't know, but, like the mall at Christmas time, it was the atmosphere he loved.

***

By this stage of Nathan's life, we were pretty much past the grieving, but shame and guilt still lurked deep in the depths of our souls, waiting for those times when our spirits were low to slink into our psyche and attack our self-worth. That happened on many occasions when people we thought were friends deserted us, when clashes with bureaucracy left us angry and frustrated, and when Nathan was ill. But seeing him as a happy child helped to banish the last vestiges of shame and guilt. When we started reading his face, at times when we were low, he did what he could do to look us in the eye and say, don't be sad for me – I am happy.

It's hard to understand the shame and the guilt. Nathan's cerebral palsy was not our fault, so we shouldn't have ever felt guilty about it, but we did, for a long time. And we loved him – well, as I pointed out, not right at the start – so why would we feel ashamed? Part of that is because of the way people reacted when they saw him. It was a little like someone with a missing limb or an ugly scar – people look away. We saw them not wanting to see our boy, it caused – or it used to cause – shame, as though he was something we should be hiding.

Getting rid of the shame and guilt was necessary for us to be realistic about what Nathan's life was going to be and plan his future. But here, in the planning, we again hit numerous obstacles. One of the biggest of these was that the world does not readily accept disabled people into the community, or accord them the same rights as everyone else. Over the time of Nathan's life, there were big changes, but there are still too many public places that don't have wheelchair access, where disabled toilets are not supplied or the needs of the disabled are not considered. Though the law stipulates that these things are required, sometimes the law is an ass, or, that is, it is made an ass by the non-compliance of authorities.

The obstacles we hit were legion, but they all had the same solution.

This is important. Are you paying attention?

Disabled people, particularly the ones that cannot speak for themselves, need an advocate. They need a good one, who is willing to speak out, to be persistent in the face of constant rebuffs, to wear down bureaucratic obstinacy. Nathan had the best advocate in the world. His mother.

Advocates have to be strong. They have to put up with abuse, trickery and procrastination from service providers and facility managers, some of whom look on the disabled as an unwanted inconvenience, somebody else's concern. They will, all too often, push advocates aside, bully them into submission, shove excuses at them, which all boil down to *nothing can be done because it's just too hard*. It requires a strong individual to hold out against this bullying.

When Nathan tried to use his Companion Card to go with his carer to a 3D movie, it created a storm that reverberated around halls of government bureaucracy. The function of the carer's card is to validate Nathan's claim that he needs a carer with him in public spaces. If it's a venue where there is a cost of entry, the carer is supposed to be admitted for free. On this occasion, when he went to a theatre that had allowed the use of his Companion Card a number of times before, his carer was told that she could not take Nathan into the movie of his choice, because it was a 3D movie, and there was too much of an expense to the management.

When Val heard this, she called the manager. She knew him, used to work with him, but that didn't stop him from attacking her like a wild thing.

'These carers just use the Companion Card to get in for free' he roared. 'I do a lot for charity. I'm doing a public service allowing its use at all.' He ranted and yelled for five minutes, shouting Val down when she tried to speak and claiming, among other things, that carers took disabled people to the movies just so they could see it for free.

What he would not acknowledge was that allowing the use of the Companion Card is not charity. It allows a disabled person to go to places a non-disabled person can go, and that is a basic human right.

It's not always bullying that the advocate has to deal with. If the evil-doers are not outright aggressive, they will be cooperatively passive in dealing with a problem, making noises like they want to help but doing nothing. Yes, they might say, it is a problem. Yes, something must be done, but...

And then one of three tactics will be employed.

They will claim that there is nothing that can be done about it. Or...

They will say that it's not their area of responsibility, that we will have to talk to someone else.

Or...

They will say that they have been trying to get so-and-so in such-and-such department to do something, and that they will try again tomorrow.

And, as the old saying goes, tomorrow never comes.

It took us over a year to get an organisation – one that had been set up solely for the purpose of offering programs to the disabled – to set up a hoist and change table so Nathan could be changed when attending programs there. Month after month the administration kept promising that things were in the pipeline, and blaming others for the slow progress. Why they didn't get one before we started nagging them, I have no idea. And then, when they finally installed one, they refused to take any responsibility for learning how to use it.

Odd. Really odd.

When services don't exist, it is necessary to talk to the evil-doers – evil because they do nothing – and convince them that the law and basic human values indicate that the service is needed. When convincing has to be done, it helps to be able to state your case clearly, concisely, and forcefully.

In Nathan's early years, we tried to get him into day care but found that none of the local organisations could take him, even though they wanted to, because he needed a full-time attendant. The day care centres did not receive funding for one-on-one care, no matter how urgent the need. Effectively, that meant every high-needs child in the state was barred from attending a day care centre. The regional office of the Department of Human Services told us that the only way to secure this funding was to go to DHS head office in Melbourne, and talk to a public servant whose brief included funding distribution for day care centres.

So, Val and some day care administrators went to Melbourne to argue the case. They were shepherded in to the office of a senior public servant. They asked her if she was responsible for equity in the distribution of funds to day care agencies.

Ms Public Servant said she was.

They argued that there was legislation that stipulated that every child had the right to attend a day care centre.

Ms Public Servant agreed.

They argued that it wasn't possible under current funding arrangements, so a number of children, one of them Ms Runyan's child, they pointed at Val, were unable to attend.

Ms Public Servant looked at Val with a condescending air. 'There's nothing I can do, but you have my sympathies,' she said.

That was a big mistake.

'Wait a minute,' Val had said – and I could just imagine how her eyes were blue chips of ice and her accusing finger inches from the woman's face – 'I am not looking for your sympathies. I don't want them. I want you to act on your obligations to arrange funding so there is equity in the distribution of day care funds. I want you to honour your obligation to ensure that every child has the right to attend a day care centre. That is your job, is it not?'

There was more. Quite a bit more. Ms Public Servant tried to argue, but she'd unleashed a force she couldn't handle. By the time Val had finished, the woman was cringing down in her chair and nodding obsequiously. The funding model was changed, for the whole state, and Nathan and a lot of other disabled kids went to day care.

Advocates need to be persistent. Pest-like persistent. Because the obstacles they hit are so numerous, I am sure that a lot of advocates burn out while pushing the cause of their charges. I would have, and I was constantly in awe of the way Val was unwavering in pushing bureaucracies to measure up to the standards set by the needs of her boy.

We were down at Port Fairy, walking along the beach, when we saw that the council had put in a set of steps, to replace a rough sandy track and improve beach access. What steamed us was that the top part of the access was a ramp, and the bottom part was steps. Now what mental giant had thought of that? What use was half a ramp to the disabled person in a wheelchair? What was the point of getting a wheelchair half way down a slope to the beach, only to hit an impassable obstacle?

Val bristled like a mastiff sensing a fight. She wrote to the council. She challenged any of the councillors of Moyne Shire to sit in a chair and propel themselves safely down the only possible disabled access – the surf club boat ramp, not the impassable ramp/steps – remain in the chair and then wheel themselves, or push another person in a wheelchair, back up the ramp. She quoted the *Disability Discrimination Act*, and after a number of communications she eventually extracted a promise that proper access would be put in. But, of course, it wasn't done. Senior figures in the Council decided that the budget wouldn't allow further expenditure on access to the beach. Val wrote again, quoting the DDA which stripped budget restraints away as an excuse for not providing beach access for the disabled. The fight went on.

And on.

And on.

As of the writing of this story we have stepped away from that fight – when fighting for a kid like Nathan you cannot fight every fight, there are just too many – but only because we've moved interstate. Should we return, and we still own our Port Fairy house, the fight will continue.

***

Part of our battle to get Nathan accepted by the wider community had been triggered by two faulty perceptions. The first one was the belief that people with Nathan's level of disability can make no meaningful contribution to society. The second was that because it's believed the Nathans of the world make no contribution to society, resources should not be wasted on them. No-one has ever pushed these perceptions into our faces, but there is no doubt that they are there – ugly, unsaid – but there.

I'm not sure who I am quoting here, but the sentiment gets it right: *Some people make the world special just by being in it.*

That was my son. He made the world special. The kid lit up a room when he entered. That was his meaningful contribution to society.

Nathan also made other contributions, particularly to his parents. He was the glue that kept Valerie and me together. We know he needed us as permanent fixtures in his life, so in those go-for-the-jugular arguments that all married couples have, we knew we had to see our way through them. I am not saying that we wouldn't have stayed together without Nathan, but he certainly made it essential.

At a personal level, he taught me to be more careful and methodical than I had been before he was born. Val insists that I am still neither of those things, but she does grant that

I improved over the years of Nathan's life. I had to. Prior to his birth I was the master of the band-aid solution. My philosophy was, whatever is wrong get it fixed as quickly as possible and any way you can. As you can imagine, this resulted in me coming up with some slipshod solutions to significant problems. And, therefore, because I hadn't fixed them properly, the problems came back. But a quick-fix philosophy doesn't work with a high-needs kid. When Nathan had a problem, it had to be fixed right, if fixable at all, and, if possible, fixed permanently. His needs were too plentiful and too multi-faceted to do it any other way.

When Nathan was 15, we were in Port Fairy for a weekend. As one always does when on vacation, we put Nathan in his running buggy and took him for a walk on the beach. About five kilometres from our house, at a place where there were no lifeguards or access roads, the back axle of the buggy broke. It was badly corroded. It had been my job over the years to hose it off to rid it of sand and salt after walks on the beach. I had done that job, religiously, but I'd done it in my usual slap-dash way, which meant I didn't take the wheels off and spray inside the axles to get rid of all the sand and salt that caused the rust that weakened the axle. My reward? An angry spouse, 40 kilos of stranded boy, a run back home to get the car, then the need to beg a passer-by for help to carry Nathan and the wounded buggy up off the beach and down to the car. In other words, a lesson in the futility of band-aid solutions.

There is also the benefit we had from Nathan's effect on our friendship circle. This benefit I haven't yet figured out. Well, I know what the benefit is, I just don't know why it happens. This was how it worked: Nathan caused people to show their true colours. We lost friends because of Nathan. That doesn't sound like a benefit, does it? There wasn't anything flawed about the friends we've lost. They just weren't very good friends, even though in some cases we thought they were.

I think they gave up on calling us, or calling by, because they got tired of playing second fiddle to Nathan's needs. They would call, invite us to dinner or to a movie or whatever, and we would say, 'No, thank you, we'd love to come but Nathan isn't well.' Or,

'Nathan has an appointment with so-and-so.' Or, 'We can't get Nathan's chair up the stairs to the restaurant you're going to.' After a while these friends stopped calling, and invitations from them dried up. Was this a benefit? Yes, if you want your friends to be people you can rely on. The benefit was that the friends that stayed with us have become all the more valued because they were loyal through the tough times, through the last-minute changes of plans, dinner cancellations, disappointments and failures to show up. They understood when we have said, 'No, thank you, we'd love to come but Nathan...' They have understood, and they have kept calling, kept inviting. They are friends we can rely on.

The other contribution that Nathan made to us was that he helped us understand that life isn't all about work, that there is a self-family-work balance. And by demanding that we spend time on him he made damned sure that we didn't let work take over our lives.

***

It would be remiss of me not to mention that we adjusted to Nathan's disability because of the kindness of people who didn't know him, who only met him in passing.

We went back up to northern New South Wales, for a Christmas celebration at my brother Paul's place, 15 km to the west of Nimbin. Paul and Jeni have 180 acres of hills, rainforest and paradise. When they bought it, shortly after the Aquarius Festival in 1973, it was a run-down dairy farm on land that was tired and depleted. Paul was one of the original hug-a-tree types, before it was in vogue to be one, and he set about restoring the land to its former glory. When we arrived for that Christmas, along with numerous other brothers, sisters, brothers and sisters-in-law, and nephews and nieces, the place was a picture. The time stands out in my memory because of the help and support we got, not only from family when we arrived, but also on the trip up and back, at every town we stopped at, every gas station, restaurant (all bar one), hotel and B&B along the way.

At a restaurant in a small town, there were some steps that had to be negotiated. When the proprietor saw Nathan's wheelchair, he offered to let us dine in the kitchen so we didn't have to get up the stairs. He brought chairs and a table into the kitchen, and sat and talked to Nathan while we ate. Then he wouldn't take any money for the meal.

At a B&B somewhere north of Bathurst, the owner came to ask Nathan if he would like to help her feed her pet kangaroos. When she heard that we were about to pack Nathan and wheelchair back into the car to go into town to buy food, she supplied us with all the food we needed from her own kitchen, and would accept no payment for it.

When we stopped in Kyogle to buy groceries, the store manager carried the groceries to our car herself, and chatted to Nathan as though he was her long lost friend. No big deal, but such a nice change from the people who stare then turn away.

This, we found, was one of the hallmarks of having a disabled child: the vast majority of people go out of their way to help. I could go on and on and on with examples of kindness from strangers. What they did, over the years, was to make small gestures of help and support. They didn't remove Nathan's disability, they didn't stop people from staring, but they made a big difference to our lives.

***

There was, on that trip, one incident that summed up the negative attitude of a very small number of people that we have encountered over the years. On the way home, we stopped in a small town on the South Coast. The sun was shining, the bulk of the road trip was behind us, we were in a good mood. Then we went into a restaurant for dinner and our good mood got shot to hell.

Just as we were sitting down a woman came running out from behind the counter, and, before she opened her mouth, we knew this was going to be one of those incidents. Every aspect of her demeanour read hostility.

'Get that out of here,' she screamed, 'you can't bring that in here.' She was pointing, gesticulating, at Nathan like he was a nasty contagion. 'You take it out or I will call the police.'

It. And *That.* My son. Referring to him like that cut me like the sharpest blade. Though I know she was talking about his wheelchair, that she saw the chair and not the person in it was equally upsetting. We tried to talk to her, then, as she continued to scream and point, we tried to argue, but to no avail. She was not going to listen.

I wish – and have wished countless times – that I'd said that, if she didn't serve us, I would call the police myself. And when the manager joined the fray, I wish I had told him, as he supported the ugly demands of his waitress, that they would serve us or we would sue. Instead, I spat the dummy. I yelled, and, though I'm not big, I've got a school teacher's voice, and everybody within half a block heard what I had to say. And, as I had a lot to say, I yelled for some time. I yelled that awful pair into silence, and then we left.

As I stalked out in high dudgeon, I noticed that not a single patron in the restaurant had moved. No-one would even look at us.

It was a nasty incident, but once Nathan reached his twenties I could think of only a few occasions when we encountered such attitudes.

***

I don't know at what point in Nathan's life it was that we accepted Nathan's disability, but I know we did. And I do know that it was not until we had fully accepted it that we were able to adjust to it. I think that we had largely – not totally – accepted what we had in Nathan very early, but we kept hoping for miracles for a long time after that. We adjusted when we fully accepted what we had, and that came after we stopped hoping for miracles.

Let's be clear on what I mean when I use these terms *accepted* and *adjusted*. We accepted Nathan's disability when we were able to say this is what we've got: a severely disabled kid. And this meant planning our lives around Nathan and his uniquities. Not an easy rethink for two people whose professional lives are a large part of their makeup.

We read an article in the newsletter for what was then the Spastic Society – horrible name, glad they changed it. It went like this:

> *Imagine that through all your life you wanted to go to Italy. You've read about it, studied the language, saved for it. Now you're ready to go.*
>
> *You buy the tickets. You study the guidebooks. You go to the airport. You get on the plane. You are so excited; it's finally happening; you're going to Italy.*
>
> *But at the other end of the trip, when you get off the plane, you find there's been a mistake. You're in France, not in Italy.*
>
> *You can spend the rest of your life regretting that you never got to Italy. But if you look around you'll see that there are some really nice things in France, things you'd never have found out about if you kept mourning that you didn't get to Italy.*

We're in France now. We never got to Italy, but France is nice. We're happy in France.

Chapter 11: The Law Suit

When Nathan was two, my brother Noel, who is a surgeon, came down to visit us.

He came to be supportive, but it didn't take Val long to put him to use. He hadn't been there for more than an hour before she had him studying some of Nathan's brain scans.

He asked us to leave him alone for a while, so he could go over them uninterrupted. When he called us in, he held one of the scans up to the light.

'You see these black spots?' he asked.

We nodded. How could we not? They were huge.

'They indicate the damaged areas of the brain,' Noel said. 'In practical terms, those black spots show us dead tissue. We can predict a lot about the nature and extent of Nate's problems by looking at the location of these spots and interpreting them in light of the part of the brain that's affected.'

Val and I stared at the picture of Nathan's brain. There were more dark spots than non-dark spots.

'That's a lot of damage,' I said.

'He must have been suffering a lot of bradycardia to get that much damage,' said Val.

'Yes,' said Noel, 'he must have.' He pointed at a large black area on the x-ray. 'This shows damage to the white matter. When the brain is suffering a shortage of oxygen it protects the areas that are needed for the body's vital functions. So, what gets sacrificed are those areas like muscle control, areas that don't actually support life.'

I waved my hand around like a kid in a school room. 'So, when he was being born, and his body was running out of oxygen, it made choices about which parts of the brain would get oxygen and which wouldn't?'

'Yes.'

Val posed the question on both our minds. 'What does this mean for his future?'

Noel scratched the back of his neck and studied the x-rays again. 'There's going to be a significant effect on his ability to move,' he said. 'That means movement of the limbs, mouth, eyes, neck, trunk etcetera will be compromised. From what I'm seeing here, it's likely that he will have little ability to react to external stimuli. He may understand what's going on around him, but he'll have limited ability to respond to it.'

Val moved over to Noel and took the x-ray from him. 'So, you agree he must have been suffering a lot of bradycardia to get that much damage.'

Noel nodded.

'Shouldn't something have been done?'

Noel nodded again.

'Shouldn't we have known? Shouldn't we have demanded they do something?' I asked.

'You wouldn't have known what bradycardia was,' said Noel.

Val turned to me. 'We're going to sue,' she said.

You hear about people getting drunk, falling over, and suing because there was a pothole in the road. You read about people staying up all night, getting into a car, crashing, and suing because the road conditions where they crashed weren't perfect. You hear stories of someone taking drugs, going surfing and then suing because their head gets smashed into a sandbank. Suing had a number of negative connotations. We'd been considering it for a while, but those bad connotations got in the way. Were we being like the drunk that fell in the pothole? Or the tired driver? Or the stupid surfer? After our talk with Noel, we stopped comparing ourselves to these people. The moral/ethical issues had been considered, and dispatched.

There were a number of reasons why we believed the hospital and the attending obstetrician were negligent.

First, there was the bradycardia that Nathan was suffering during labour. I didn't think much about it at the time, mainly because, as Noel pointed out, I didn't know what it was, but also because I was so sure that the experts who were attending to

Val would be doing their jobs properly. I did notice though that the midwives were concerned enough about it to send for the doctor a number of times. But every time they called, they were told he was in a meeting and could not be disturbed. He didn't come to see Val until she had been in labour for about 15 hours. Prior to that one visit, when he decided that Val would have a caesarean, instead of coming and checking on her himself the doctor sent instructions for Val to be given doses of syntocin. Syntocin facilitates labour when there is an inadequate uterine effort, but it is not supposed to be given if there is evidence of foetal distress, which there was in Nathan's birth.

Second was the actual birth. During the caesarean operation, a screen blocked me from seeing the lower half of Val's body. In hindsight, that screen tells me that somebody knew that there was a likelihood of a bad outcome. One they didn't want me to see.

Third, two days after the birth we were told by one of the nurses in the maternity ward that the head administrator had called in every staff member that had been involved in Nathan's case. She told them to document everything that had happened. They were told to do it very carefully, and to submit their notes to the hospital administration. There was a bad outcome at Nathan's birth, no-one can argue with that, but at the time no-one would admit anything had gone wrong. Why, one wonders, were they so concerned if nothing had gone wrong?

***

We found the name of a law firm in Sydney that specialised in medical negligence cases. We flew to Sydney, talked to them, gave them all the records we had, and promised to send the rest from home. By this time, Val, who saves every receipt, invoice, bank transaction and record that ever passes through her hands, had a boatload of Nathan-related files.

Our law suit was under way.

It took nearly ten years and 60,000 dollars for it to crash and burn, but, eventually, it did.

The biggest single expense was the medical experts, who looked at Nathan's records and interpreted them. The only way to look at what some of these experts did is to say that they were bloody dishonest. There is no other explanation for the fact that there were so many different interpretations of Nathan's case. I think that some of these professionals saw giving opinions on medical negligence cases as an easy way to make money. They simply closed ranks to protect their own, gave an opinion, and took the money anyway.

The most blatant example of their dishonesty was the bloke who said that there was no negligence, that Nathan's outcome was a result of the knot in his umbilical cord. There was no knot in his umbilical cord.

That so-called expert looked at Nathan's birth record – clearly, he did not look at it closely enough – and saw that there was a tick in the box beside the words 'knot in umbilical cord'. The best excuse I can give that person is that the form was poorly designed.

At the top of the form it said, 'Tick if no problems were encountered'. No problems with a knot in the umbilical cord were encountered because there was no knot, so whoever filled in the form put a tick in the appropriate box.

Now I grant you that this is open to misinterpretation. If you don't look at the form carefully, you don't notice the instruction at the top. But the guy was paid thousands for his opinion, and for that fee he bloody well should have looked closely enough to complete the questions properly.

In the end, an expert came up with an interpretation that had not been mentioned by any of the previous experts, an interpretation that could not be refuted because there was no way of proving or disproving it. This expert said that Nathan's outcome was a result of a virus, unnamed, hitherto unmentioned and undetected, that Val had contracted some time immediately before giving birth.

The lawyers did their best. They sent Nathan's records to ten different experts. None of them said anything similar to the one before or the one after. Two of them supported our case, but not in a very strong way. The issue of the syntocin being administered when it was contraindicated because Nathan was in foetal distress, somehow didn't matter. It wasn't mentioned in any of the reports.

We were angry when we decided to give it up. But eventually, we decided to put the anger behind us. We were not going to live with that for the rest of our lives.

Part 4: Living With Nathan

Chapter 12: The Great Nate Titanium Tait

Between the ages three and ten Nathan had three operations – one for the removal of tonsils and adenoids, and two to fix his hips.

The tonsils and adenoids had to go because they were interfering with Nathan's breathing. The muscle tone in his throat was poor, and the removal of organs he didn't really need helped to clear his airways.

There is always some risk when a person is given an anaesthetic and instruments intrude into the body, but with a cerebral palsy kid the risk is higher, so it was with some trepidation when we went to the Royal Children's Hospital to have Nathan's tonsils taken out. But he came through like a champion, and afterwards the surgeon said he was surprised at how quickly Nathan recovered.

'He seems to have some fighting qualities,' the surgeon said, confirming what I already knew about any child that came from my loins. His fighting qualities meant a speedy recovery and we were able to go home much earlier than originally anticipated.

The second operation, when Nathan was five, was to fix his hips. The femurs were dislocating from the sockets in the pelvic girdle. It happens frequently in cerebral palsy kids, because the pull of the muscles in different parts of the body is so uneven, and in Nathan's case he was unable to offset this uneven pull, by standing or through any form of stretching or exercise. If we didn't treat this problem, it would get worse and worse, and though he was never going to walk anyway, it would have led to him suffering pain just from sitting.

When he came out of the operation, he was in what is called a spika: a cast from hips to ankles, with legs spread wide, a bar between the calves and a gap for his bum so he could poo. Because the cast came so far up his waist, a choice had to be made about whether Nathan would be in the sitting position, or prone for the period the cast was in place. For lung and chest reasons, prone was not recommended, so Nathan was in a sitting position for the three months that the cast was on his body.

He was just a tiny little guy at that stage, so moving him around in his spika was easy. There was only one problem, and that was his bowels.

If you've ever had an operation where the amount of sedative is quite large for your body, you'll know that there is likely to be a heavy 'binding' effect. For Nathan, he was bound for days. He still hadn't pooed when everything else was sailing so smoothly that, when we were asked if we wanted to go home, which came about more quickly than expected, or wait until Nathan let loose, we didn't spend much time thinking about it. Hospital was hospital; home was home. We chose to go home.

We went home, with our bound boy in a powder blue hip spika, and we waited for his bowels to open.

And waited.

And waited.

All the time we were waiting, we were giving him prune juice, Agarol, Senokot and various other laxatives. It seemed like he stayed bound forever.

If this doesn't seem like a big deal to you, just consider: he'd had both femurs broken and the shafts of the femurs rotated so the ball at the top of the bone fitted into the socket better. He was unable to move his lower extremities. He was unable to tell us about any discomfort he was suffering, and you can be sure that with all the laxatives we were giving him he was suffering something awful.

When he finally cut loose, thank God I had a friend in the house to help me. We held Nathan up from his bed with each of us holding an arm and an ankle encased in a powder blue cast. The poo flowed from him in an unending stream. I can only imagine how he was feeling.

The second hip operation was carried out because the first operation was only partially successful, and the breaking of femurs and rotating of balls into sockets had to be done again. This time though, the operation itself wasn't so problem free.

Somehow or other, the spinal tap put into his spine to administer pain medication didn't work, and the little kid spent several days screaming, crying and moaning through every waking moment. There are few things that cause a parent more stress than seeing an offspring in pain. Nathan's parents went berserk with worry, and hounded the poor bloody hospital staff to distraction. The medical team eventually concluded that the spinal tap must not have been in the right position. They moved it, just a fraction, so the medication dripped unimpeded into the spinal cord.

The orthopaedic specialist overseeing both of these operations was Professor Kerr Graham. If ever there was a saint in earthly form it is Kerr Graham. Whenever Nathan was in pain, I think Prof Graham was too. When Nathan's operations were successful, Kerr Graham was every bit as delighted as his parents. The guy was really competent, and he really cared.

***

For the first five years of Nathan's life, our days were dominated by specialists. There were a host of different doctors and therapists, a multitude of educators and who knows how many social workers. Then, for a few years, after his hip operations and as we adjusted to the realities of Nathan's condition, the flood of information, advice and predictions eased and our lives took on a level of stability. But in the late 1990s, Nathan started to develop some spinal problems, and the specialists entered our lives again.

The technical names for his spinal problems were kyphosis and lordosis. In practical terms, it meant his spine was curving out to the right near the top, and to the left lower down. It was also bowing out, hunchback style, near the top.

As always happened when we wanted to see a medical specialist, we had to go through channels and jump through hoops. Our starting point was our local paediatrician, who directed us back to Professor Kerr Graham – may the saints praise his holy name – at the Royal Children's hospital. Kerr Graham told us that spines were not his area of specialisation. He referred us to the hospital's spinal specialist.

For reasons that neither Val or I understood, this guy refused to do the operation. He was a spinal specialist at the Royal Children's Hospital. Nathan was a child with a spinal problem. What, we wondered, set him apart from the other children that needed spinal surgery?

'Just take him home and love him,' said the specialist.

But just taking him home and loving him meant watching him over the years while his spine twisted further until it eventually collapsed. Just taking him home and loving him meant condemning him to a life of increasing pain. We were not, not, not going to allow that to happen.

There was never the smallest iota of doubt that Nathan needed that surgery. It had already been a couple of years since the problems had first been detected, and by the time the specialist had made his ridiculous, pompous, unhelpful statement, the curvature of the spine was cramping Nathan's gut, lungs and diaphragm. One lung was being squeezed so much it had, effectively, ceased working. If we hadn't done something to take pressure off the spine and stop it from deforming further, it could have killed him.

Kerr Graham was really pissed off that this guy wouldn't do the surgery. Kerr Graham is a man who fights for what he believes, and he believed that Nathan needed the operation. He, and we, didn't want the reluctant surgeon to do this operation, because a reluctant surgeon might be off his game just a tad when working on a case he didn't want to work on. So, we didn't try to talk the fool around – we looked elsewhere.

Elsewhere turned out to be Michael Johnson, a spinal surgeon at the Monash Medical Centre. Michael agreed to do the operation, and told us that we would be contacted when he, the relevant staff, and the operating theatre space were all available. And that could be any time between a few weeks and six months.

We went to our different bosses at Federation University and told them what was happening in our lives. That we would get a call one day, and that we would have to book Nathan into the hospital the next. That the operation and recovery time would be about six weeks. Both of them understood and were supportive. In my case, it meant leaving in the middle of the semester, with other staff having to cover all my lectures and tutorials. They were, thank God, all willing to help.

The operation was a risky one. In fact, it was a risky two. There would be one operation where Nathan's bottom two ribs were taken out. These were to be made into a cement that would seal the rod in place and encourage bone growth around it. The second operation would be the actual tying and gluing of the rod to the spine.

It was, we were told, a rather revolutionary procedure. Because Nathan was so small the surgical team couldn't put in the usual two rods down each side of his spine. They could only use one rod, which had to be stapled top and bottom to the spine, and the rib paste put along the spine to encourage bone growth that would eventually mean the rod was entirely encased bone.

The first operation was the easy part, and it went smoothly. But, when they finally let us in to see Nathan in Intensive Care, oh brother, what a shock it was.

He was hooked up to so many wires and tubes and electrodes and I-don't-know-what things that you had to peer through a mass of stuff just to see him. There was a computer screen that showed heart rate, blood oxygen levels, blood pressure, body temperature, and respiration levels. We spent the next few days with our eyes glued to that screen.

Nathan also had his own personal nurse. Actually, he had a number of them, but one of them, the one he had when he first went into IC, became our friend. Her name was Susan, and she was a competent, caring sweetheart.

Nathan didn't get to leave IC between the two operations, and when he went into theatre for the second one, as he was wheeled towards the operating theatre, Dr Michael Johnson was outside in the corridor, on his way to scrub up.

'We're ready for the big one,' he said, with scant regard for the butterflies that were lurching around in my stomach.

'Good luck,' I said.

Val was appalled. 'No, not good luck,' she said, and it was clear from her voice that she too was stressed. 'Good management. You make sure you manage this well.'

It was a six-hour operation. I don't know what we did for those six hours, but whatever it was it didn't involve eating, sleeping or light and happy chatter. We did breathe, but we had to keep reminding each other to do even that. It wasn't until Michael Johnson came out to tell us that the operation was a success that I felt the ache in my neck and the stiffness in my shoulders.

When we finally saw Nathan back in IC, we decided to rename him Zipper. He had stitches going from the base of his spine to his neck, and two more long lines of the them winding around his chest where he'd had his bottom ribs removed in the first operation. In the spine-to-neck wound, the stitches were actually staples, over 200 little aluminium things. When he woke up, he was going to be in a world of pain like he'd never been in before, so he was zonked about as heavily as he could have been zonked.

Doctor Johnson told us that the operation had gone well. 'But,' he said, 'it will be a couple of days before he's out of the woods.'

Out of the woods. That was a nice way of saying that it would be some time before we knew if Nathan would survive. We went back to not eating, not sleeping, watching the monitors, and breathing when we remembered to. Susan, we noticed, was a lot more attentive to Nathan's progress than she was after the first operation.

About 20 hours after that second operation, something seemed to go wrong. The monitor that showed Nathan's heart rate stopped working. There had been a little line, bouncing across the screen, that showed each heartbeat, and the line stopped bouncing. Susan hit a button, and IC staff came from everywhere.

Val and I are, I would modestly claim, reasonably intelligent people. We had watched ER, we knew what flat-lining was, and to us it looked like Nathan was flat-lining: that his heart had stopped beating.

I cannot tell you how I felt. My little kid, who had been through so much, and now his heart had stopped beating. Oh shit! Oh God! Oh shit!

We were assured that Nathan was okay, but then we were asked to leave the ward. They needed to take an x-ray, they said, and it was standard procedure not to have anybody that wasn't needed standing around when there were x-rays being taken. This confirmed our worst fears. Nathan had taken a number of x-rays while he'd been in IC, and they hadn't asked us to leave before.

We went out into the corridor. We stared into space. We sobbed uncontrollably.

It wasn't necessary, though. He survived. His lungs had collapsed, but un-collapsing them was a simple procedure. It had been a dicey moment, but, like a car going into a skid with an experienced driver at the wheel, corrections were made and the dicey moment passed.

'All his vitals came back on track very nicely,' said Susan. 'Obviously our little man wants to live, and he's got the fighting spirit to make sure he gets what he wants.'

'Is he still in any danger?' asked Val.

'He's not out of danger yet,' said Susan, 'but he cleared an obstacle just now, and he's moving in the right direction.'

Again, we went back to not eating, not sleeping, watching the monitors, and breathing when we remembered to do so.

Some hours later – it must have been a lot of hours, but in a situation like that time doesn't have the same meaning – I was talking to my boy, telling him about the news, world events and, of course, sport. By now, he was on a reduced amount of drugs and we were waiting for him to emerge from the land of Zonk. That emergence was going to tell us that he was going to survive.

'Collingwood has a big game this weekend you know,' I told him. 'Nathan Buckley says that...'

He woke up, and he smiled at me.

I recalled Houston Rocket's coach Rudi Tomjanovich's advice: 'Don't ever underestimate the heart of a champion.'

I think there's a lesson for the ages here. I mean... I was talking about our team, about Collingwood, and he woke up. And just like that he'd turned the corner. He was on the mend.

Over the next few weeks Nathan had regular visits from so many specialists I lost count. I didn't know who was going to approach his bed next, and, when they came, I couldn't remember them from the last time. Except one: Spandex Lady.

Spandex Lady was drop dead gorgeous. She wore tight, stretchy outfits that showed off her shapely figure beautifully. Spandex Lady was a gut or stomach or intestinal specialist. She came with a whole team, but I'm buggered if I can remember a face, a name or specialisation of any of the others. I got to looking forward to her visits every morning. As she examined Nathan, I would search for witty things to say so I could bask in the warmth of her perfect smile. But one morning, while I was being witty and clever and I was sure she was charmed by my repartee, she interrupted me and said, 'Your child is undernourished.'

Undernourished? How could he be undernourished? We would put aside an hour for each meal, and we were very careful in ensuring that his diet was good. The problem, apparently, wasn't Nathan's diet, or the amount of time that was spent feeding him. The problem was his inability to get his mouth to do the things that were needed to take food off the spoon, form it into a bolus, and swallow. It was a slow and laborious process just to get a spoonful of food into his mouth. Getting him to swallow it was a hit-and-miss proposition. The little guy would end up with food all over his face and on the napkin that was positioned to protect his shirt. Sometimes we felt like just tossing the food onto his napkin and saying, 'there, he's had his meal.'

Even if the information had come from somebody not quite so gorgeous it still would have been hard to refute, but Spandex Lady laid the evidence out carefully and I was ready to listen to anything she said. What she said was that she had analysed Nathan's age and body length, and found his weight was too low for that age and body length, and, because he was undernourished, he was more prone to illness and infections.

'Quite aside from that,' said Spandex lady, 'he's probably hungry all the time he's awake.'

That statement really moved my attention from her body to what she was saying.

'We spend so much time trying to get food into him,' I said. 'The only way we could spend more time on it is if we don't go to work.'

'He needs a stomach peg,' said Spandex Lady.

Val and I had discussed a stomach peg a number of times, but we'd rejected the idea because we didn't want to take the joy of tasting food out of Nathan's life. But the joy of tasting food was outweighed by the likelihood of him being hungry all the time. Plans were changed, and by the time Nathan went home he had a little valve in his stomach that enabled us to fill a syringe with a specially prepared substance that we got out of a can, and squirt it straight into the valve and into his stomach.

When Nathan recovered from the surgery, under the stomach feed regime, which meant a perfectly balanced diet, he put on weight, his complexion cleared up, and those long and frustrating feeding times – three meals, plus morning and afternoon tea, close to four hours each day – were taken out of our lives. We still, for the next few years, gave Nathan some food orally, because he enjoyed the tastes that we all enjoy, chocolate, mashed potatoes with heaps of butter, ice cream, fruit flavoured yogurt. But when he was 15, we found that, with every mouthful that went into his mouth, some of the food ended up in his lungs instead of his stomach. This increased the likelihood of him contracting a lung infection. No more oral feeds. The taste of food was added to the long list of things, that we all accept as normal components of living, that Nathan misses out on.

Nathan was in hospital for about six weeks. The last thing done before we took him home was the removal of the staples from his body. We kept the staples for a while, and put them with the bolts and screws that had been inserted into his hips in those earlier hip operations. Over the years, the kid carried so much metal in him we gave him the nickname Titanium Tait. The Great Nate Titanium Tait.

We took him home, as we always did, as soon as we were able to, which was, really, much too soon.

He went home in an ambulance because he was still hooked up to various monitors, feeder tubes and catheters. When we got him home, we moved his bed into our bedroom so we could stay on top of any problems he might have during the night. By day we went back to work, and had carers by his bed all day. The district nurse called in every day to check on him and the various drip bottles that held drugs, fluids and nutrition. Nathan had to be suctioned to get the gunk from his lungs out when he coughed enough to get the gunk up into his throat. And he had to be turned regularly so he didn't get bed sores. It was tedious. The tedium didn't come from looking after the little invalid though; it came from having so many strangers in the house for so long.

That recovery period was hard work, but we were home. And the little kid's back problem was fixed.

Chapter 13: A Typical Day

Like all kids, Nathan was growing up and he wasn't going to get to stay at school forever. After six pleasant years at Ballarat Special School, it was time for him to move out into the world. There was a number of organisations that provided programs for the disabled, and one night we went to an information session where different organisations spruiked their wares and answered question from parents. The other parents of Special School leavers probably felt like we did, that, because their children had few life skills and limited physical capability, their future was like a venture onto a wide ocean on a rudderless raft.

Some of the organisations offered such a diverse range of services that you could take your kid there in the morning and leave him/her there all day. The organisation would take care of the program, lunch, changing, social activity and learning. We looked into them, we went to their premises, we talked to administrators and program managers. The three of us decided that they weren't what we wanted. They were all too institutional. They looked, smelt and sounded like institutions for the afflicted. Undoubtedly, they all did good jobs – they just weren't right for Nathan.

Val decided that she was going to develop his program. She would pick and choose from everything that was available, and construct what she wanted that wasn't there. After much pushing, shoving, begging and cajoling, she developed a program that, for the next few years, read as follows:

Monday, he went to a film-making class;

Tuesday, music;

Wednesday, acting;

Thursday, art.

Friday was Nathan's community service day, when he went to Creswick, picked up mail from the post office and delivered it to businesses along the main street. He got to be quite well known in Creswick.

To one not familiar with the world of the disabled, questions arise about how? How does a boy who can't talk or move around involve himself in an acting class? If he can't use his arms or hands, how does he get anything out of an art class? How does a kid that can't respond to external stimuli demonstrate an appreciation of music?

Well, he does all of the above.

Let's look at what's happened in art. He had an easel that was remodelled to suit his needs, and a paintbrush on an extension strapped to his hand. One day he took a photo of orangutans to class, taken on our trip to Borneo where Nathan had a face-to-face, touching distance, meeting with a young orangutan named Reggie. Armed with Reggie's photograph, Nathan chose his paint colours, and refused all input from the teachers. The carer helped him to get the brush onto the paper, and Nathan painted. His concentration was intense. Over the next two weeks the movements of the brush became more frequent and more purposeful. He was painting orangutans. His choice of colour? Brown, every week while he was painting from that photo.

Did he know what he was doing? Was he trying to portray what he saw in the picture and remembered from our trip? An expert would be non-committal; his parents are absolutely convinced.

This is not the only evidence we have that Nathan knew what was going on in his classes, that he was interested and that he wanted to be part of the action. There was enough evidence for us to engage Nathan with a weekly program and a daily schedule that was highly structured. It helped him to understand where he was going and what was going to happen on any particular day.

Although it varied, his daily routine looked like this:

Six o'clock was getting up time. If Nathan was awake when I got up, there was usually something wrong, and he'd let me know. Not something drastically wrong, just something that needed attention. He'd hear me moving around, and he would start calling.

His call said *pay attention to me.*

I'd go into his room, bid him good morning, and take my first cue from how he looked and sounded. He didn't move around much, at night or any other time, but sometimes he would move enough for a limb to be hanging over the side of the bed. Or maybe he needed to be changed. Or maybe he was drooling heavily and the towel under his head was saturated and he wanted it changed.

Val and I were chuffed when we realised there was a relation between him hollering out and his perception that there was a problem. It was one of the concrete signs that his noise making wasn't just noise making, it was him communicating. Did it mean that, whenever he vocalised, which was a cross between a chortle and a yell, that he was communicating? Yes, we think it so. Did he always know what he was trying to communicate, or was he just letting us know that he was feeling some kind of feeling that was strong enough that he wanted to express that he was feeling it? Maybe, sometimes, he was just vocalising because he could. But there was no doubt that, at other times, he was communicating a message that, in his mind, was quite clear.

Once he had been been checked, and assuming there was nothing major that needed attention, he got to sleep a little longer.

Seven o'clock was time for Nathan's medication and getting ready to face the day. He had five different medicines in the morning: Epilim, Frisium and Lamictal for epilepsy; Losec to decrease the acidity of his stomach so his reflux didn't burn his oesophagus; Movicol to keep his bowels moving. The meds were dissolved in 300 ml of water and injected through his peg. As the first step in getting him out of bed, Nathan was checked for bowel movements. If necessary, his catheter condom and/ or disposable shield was replaced. If the worst happened, and he'd had a condom failure during the night, he would have a sponge bath and I would change his waterproof sheet protector. His catheter bag was emptied, re-taped to his leg, and the valve at the bottom checked to ensure it was closed. On a few occasions – very few, it's the kind of mistake you should only make once – someone forgot to close the valve at the bottom of the catheter bag and we had an accident like the one in the bar in Los Angeles.

This all took about an hour.

At 8 p.m., Nathan got dressed. So simple for those of whole bodies and minds. For Nathan, because the musculature of his hands, arms and shoulders was so tight, getting his clothes on was a wrestle. The pants had to be put on while he was still on the bed. He was rolled from side to side while they were inched up over his hips. His shirt and sweater were put on when he was in the wheelchair, while I talked him through the whole procedure. 'I'm going to roll you round to get your pants on Nate.' And, 'I'm going get you into your chair so we can put your shirt on.' And so on. If he was moved suddenly or unexpectedly, he'd get a shitty look on his face to show his disapproval.

How we got him into his wheelchair depended on who was doing it. Most days I would lift him manually off the bed and into his chair. We had a sling and a hoist, which Val and the carers who inhabited our house used, but I preferred to lift him myself. As long as I could lift Nathan, and walk a short distance with him, holidays like our trips to Fiji, Costa Rica and Borneo were possible, so I had to keep in practice.

Once he was in his wheelchair, orthotics were put on his calves and feet to help limit lower leg contractions. His shoes were put over them.

At 8.30 a.m., Nathan's carer would arrive. (We were funded by the government for about 30 hours of care per week. Without that funding, surviving would have been hard for us. This all changed for the better when the much-publicised National Disability Insurance Scheme became a reality). The carer took charge of brushing Nathan's teeth, washing his face, and cleaning his hands, which were permanently clenched and susceptible to fungus infections. If we were a bit careless with the hand washing duty, we soon got alerted by the odour that emanated from his tightly bunched fists.

Before he left the house, he was given a can of the formula through his tummy peg. He was given more water with the formula.

At 9 a.m., Nathan and carer left the house for the first of his classes. He traveled in his own car, which was adapted to hold a wheelchair. This car was a blessing. It meant that Val or any of the carers could get Nathan and out of the car easily, without lifting him out of the wheelchair. Before we acquired the car, I took him to all his classes in mine, lifted him from chair to car, and out of my car and back into the chair at the other end. And I had to be there at the end of the class to go through the whole process again. This tied me down a bit, and without the cooperation of the timetabler at the university I could never have done it.

From 9.30 a.m. until noon, Nathan had classes: acting, film-making, music or art. He got formula or water at regular intervals throughout the day. His catheter bag was checked and emptied regularly.

In the afternoon, he had massage or hydrotherapy. His masseur's name was Grant. Grant cared for Nathan for 15 years. He massaged him, developed stretching and hydro programs and administered them. He knew Nathan like his own kids. We thought very highly of Grant.

By 4 p.m., Nathan was back home, then laid on his bed, and his catheter bag emptied. Undressed, he was taken in his hoist into the bathroom, lowered into a bathchair placed in the bath – not your normal bath, a triangular spa bath that was installed for him. But once he was too big for me to put him in it or get him out, he had a shower. The condom was taken off during the shower, and afterwards his penis was inspected for the lesions that sometimes appeared as a result of it being encased in latex all day. I could only imagine how painful those lesions were, especially if there was a condom glued over them.

After the shower, assuming a healthy penis, his catheter condom was replaced, the cleaned catheter bag re-taped to his leg and the valve at the bottom checked. If there was a problem with the penis, the condom was left off and a shield and booster pad used instead. When that happened, every two hours he would be taken from his chair and put on a bed or couch, his shield checked and changed if necessary.

Then he was dressed and hoisted, or lifted by me back into his wheelchair. Orthotics would be put on his arms to try to limit contractions. Unlike the lower leg orthotics, these were difficult to put on because of the tightness of his arms. It was hard to get them in the right position, and it caused him a bit of pain to have his arms stretched out in the fitting process. They stayed on for one or two hours depending on how well he tolerated them.

At 5 p.m. Nathan would have a meal through his peg. The carer would leave. Nathan supervised me while I cooked dinner.

By 6 p.m. Val would arrive home. After dinner, Nathan got his medication. Epilim, Frisium and Lamictal for epilepsy; Losec for his stomach. His catheter bag was checked, and the valve at the bottom double-checked.

From 7 p.m., he would watch TV from his big leather recliner, which is stationed in front of the television. It was a big screen TV, donated to him by the Starlight Foundation, along with a surround-sound system and DVD player. He liked watching sport – no prizes for guessing where that preference came from – and the country music channel. Neither Val or I are particularly into country music. He picked up that interest by himself,

One more peg feed before bed.

His bed time was decided by how tired he was. His sleeping patterns were very irregular. Sometimes he would stay awake all night and sleep all day. Because of the tightness of his musculature he burnt a lot of energy, and that was tiring for him so he slept for more hours than a non-disabled boy of the same age. If the epileptic fits had been bad, he would be very tired.

He usually went to bed between eight and ten p.m. I lifted him from his wheelchair and laid him on his bed. Five nights out of seven I would lay him on his left side. The deformity of his spine meant he slept uncomfortably on his right side. I would un-tape the catheter bag from his leg and attach a second overnight bag with larger capacity to the valve of the day bag. I'd check his condom to ensure it was going to work properly. Failures meant the condom came off and the bed got wet.

I'd spend a little time saying good night. I'd tell him to sleep well, I love him, I'd see him in the morning. Always, lurking at the fringes of my mind, was the thought that maybe I wouldn't.

Having to go through this routine was something we no longer thought about. We did not long to be shook of it, because to be shook of it would require Nathan not to be there. Family and friends offered to take Nathan, for a day, a night, a weekend, but we' preferred have the little bloke around, so we declined most of the offers until they stopped coming.

We went on two holidays without him. When he was four, we went sailing in the Whitsundays. As much as we wanted to include Nathan in everything, taking him on a yacht was not on. When he was 11, we went for a holiday in Vanuatu. Brother Roger came down from Sydney for that one. He brought guitars and bongos with him, and from what we heard when we came home, Nathan didn't miss us at all. He had a great time jamming every day with his uncle.

Part 5: Things Go Right, Things Go Wrong

Chapter 14: The Accident

When you care for a Nathan, you have to be on full alert all the time. We've heard about, read about, talked to parents of kids that are 24-hour dynamos of activity and potential destruction. Nathan was not like that, but that doesn't mean you didn't have to pay attention to him, like a hawk, all the time.

We've compared our lot to that of the parents with these dynamos. Would it be that different if Nathan was one of them, instead of a non-mover?

Not really.

The difference must be something like this: the carer of the dynamo is akin to a soldier on a battlefield, where it's all action and danger from every which way and peril and potential injuries come from everywhere. The carer of the non-mover is a soldier on sentry duty, alert to every danger. Nothing happens, yet the eyes dare not close, the attention may not waver.

The dynamos' parents are like the light cavalry. Instant decisions, move fast, get here get there, intercept, activity, escape. We, on the other hand, were the heavy cavalry. Planning, organising, lots of equipment to take every time we upped and moved. We never got to move quickly – decisions needed to be pondered. Poor planning or inattention was punished heavily.

There was one time, when for the briefest of moments my attention wavered, and it nearly resulted in Nathan's death. You've heard the expression 'break out in a cold sweat'? It seems there's something different about my metabolism. When something happens that makes others break out in a cold sweat, I get hot and flushed. And, when I think back on this incident, I still get hot and flushed. If the outcome had been different, I would never have been able to forgive myself.

In the spring after Nathan's back operation, we bought a holiday house in Port Fairy. It had been on the market for years, and it was in such a bad state that there had been no interest until we came along.

We had to work hard to get our little weatherboard cottage into a liveable state, but the effort was worthwhile. When we had finished the inside and turned our attention to the exterior, we found that, underneath piles of rubbish, waste and detritus, there was a little courtyard paved with curved red bricks. There was an old rock flowerbed, and a couple of steps carved out of limestone that led to nowhere. Very, very nice.

Port Fairy is a village of about four or five thousand people, nestled on a headland where the Moyne River empties into Bass Strait. It's one of the oldest towns and the second oldest port in Australia. It used to be called New Belfast, and you don't have to be an Einstein to figure out that its early population was largely Irish. The historical ambience of the town is one of the main attractions for visitors, and though the developers have done what they can to ruin it, the efforts of a chunk of the townsfolk to preserve this ambience are to be applauded. There are no fast-food franchises, no poker machines. The highest building in town is two levels. Street front facades have to be maintained when renovations are carried out on the old houses. Very, very nice.

In November 2008, when Nathan was 18, Val went on a business trip to the US. Nate and I decided to take our two dogs down to Port Fairy for a boys' weekend. We arrived on a Friday night. I don't remember what we did on Saturday, so it must have been an uneventful day. Sunday started out that way too. Unfortunately, Sunday didn't finish that way.

Somewhere around 10 a.m., I put Nathan in his beach buggy, and he, the dogs and I went for a walk.

Pushing the beach buggy and a 55 kilo boy along the beach wasn't that easy. Sometimes the sand is firm and the buggy rolls along like skates on ice. This time the sand was soft. It was like pushing through sticky goo that clung at the wheels and made the going slow and hard. When we turned off the beach, onto the walk by the river, I was feeling a bit blown.

To the right of the walk is bush and shrubbery, on the left is the river. The walkway itself is a metre-and-a-half wide concrete walk. Feeling a bit buggered, I steered the buggy onto the concrete walk close to the river. Then I turned to call the two dogs to heel, and in that brief moment I put a wheel of the buggy over the edge of the walk.

As the buggy tipped towards the river, I tried for one frantic moment to heave it up straight, but I couldn't. Nathan fell from the buggy, tumbled down three metres of bluestone clinkers and into the river.

Nathan's muscle tone was very tight. That means that his arms were hard against his chest, almost in the pose of a boxer with his guard held low. He could not move his arms from where they were locked by cerebral palsy affected muscles. As he tumbled down those rocks, he couldn't use them to break his fall or protect his face. The memory of him falling out of the buggy, striking his left shoulder on the rocks, tipping up onto his face, sliding down the rocks, flipping from front to back to front and into the water, is indelibly etched in my mind.

From the moment of the wheel going over the edge, to him splashing into the water, must have been about three or four seconds. When the vision unwinds before my eyes, I relive every hit of Nathan's body, every scrape of his skin on the rocks, every detail, every millisecond. If the film in my memory was a guide you would think that it took minutes for him to fall from the buggy to the water.

If I did anything right at that time it was that I kept my composure. I was down into the water almost as soon as Nathan disappeared under the surface, and I had his face out of the water before he had a chance to inhale much at all. He did inhale a little bit. Just a little. But, oh, what problems that little bit of inhaled water was to create.

Nathan was hollering something fierce, and with good reason. His forehead, from temple to temple, was raw and bloody; his left eye was swollen and half-closed; he was shaking like a leaf in a breeze, though whether from the shock or the cold water I don't know. I tried to lift him out of the water and climb back up the slope, but with his clothes sodden and the steepness of the slope, I couldn't do it. I tried again. No way.

The gear that had been in the buggy – pillows, baseball caps, blanket, doggy pooh bags – was all bobbing away with the tide. I looked around to signal for help. There was none in sight. I pulled my mobile phone from my waterlogged pocket and opened it. The screen gave one brief flash, and died.

One of my two dogs, a Springer Spaniel called Stanley, was down there in the water with us. He wanted to help. He was barking and whimpering, but he wasn't quite up to doing a Rex The Wonder Dog thing, so, other than being concerned and being there he wasn't much use. The other dog, Little, a Maltese Terrier, had his nose stuck over the edge of the walk, looking down at us with great concern. He wasn't going to come down into that cold water though, no way, and, anyway, like Stanley, he wouldn't have been much help.

I'm not sure how long we were there – five or twenty minutes, I don't know. But finally a boatload of fishermen saw our plight and came to help. It seemed to me that they came awfully slowly, and were unduly concerned about not getting their feet wet in jumping from boat to land, but that's probably unfair, and probably more a picture in my fevered imagination than in reality. Anyway, they got there, and three of them helped me to pull Nathan and the buggy back up the slope to safety.

We put Nathan into the buggy. He was wet through, shivering, hurting, crying. Both of his eyes were turning black. The abrasions across his forehead were bleeding profusely and the blood was running down his face and turning the top of his shirt a bright watery red. Like his forehead, the knuckles on both hands were scraped raw and bleeding.

'Are you alright?' one of the fishermen asked me.

'Yeah, I'm okay,' I said, 'but my boy...' I gestured towards Nathan and started blubbering.

'He'll be alright,' said the fisherman, though we both knew he was just saying the right thing. 'We've called for an ambulance. It'll be here soon.'

We started towards Battery Point, which was where the

riverside walk finishes and is the nearest point to a road. One of the buggy's axles had bent, we had to half roll half carry it. As we neared Battery Point, a police car arrived, driving slowly up the narrow walk between river and scrub. The two cops were, as you would expect of small-town policemen, amiable blokes who wanted to do whatever needed to be done to help. They loaded Nathan in the front seat, bundled him in a blanket, and backed up to Battery Point where we met the ambulance. While Nathan and I were taken to the Port Fairy Hospital, the two dogs and the lame buggy were loaded into the back of the divvy van and taken back to our house.

In the hospital, doctors and nursing staff did all the right things. They got Nathan out of his wet clothes and wrapped him in heated blankets. They tended to the wounds on his face, checked him for concussion, took x-rays to look for broken or cracked bones in his skull and to see if he had inhaled water into his lungs. They gave him sedatives and painkillers. Finally, they sent me home to change, because, apart from being blubbery about what I had done to my boy, I was dripping all over the emergency room floor.

'We need a contact number,' said the nurse, 'in case we need to get hold of you.'

'I don't have one,' I replied. 'My phone took a dunking.'

'If you're going to leave here, we need a contact number,' said the nurse. 'Do you know any of your neighbours?'

I asked her to look up a name in the phone book, she did, and got my neighbour's number, and I left to let the neighbour know. But when I got around to his place, I couldn't go inside. Every time I tried to think of what I was going to say I fell apart like a sooky boy.

Think about it. What could I say?

'Hi Franco. I just dropped Nathan in the river and he's in hospital. Can I use you as an emergency contact?'

A bit dramatic.

'Hi, Franco. I dropped by to see if I can I use you as an emergency contact?'

That raised more questions than were being asked.

'Hi, Franco. Nathan's in hospital. Can I use you as an emergency contact?'

That avoided the issue of why he was in hospital and his stupid bloody father's part therein.

In the end, I didn't tell Franco, though he's a good friend, but I should have. I borrowed a mobile from another neighbour, without telling him what had happened to Nathan and after I concocted a story about losing my own phone. When I left his house, I called him on his landline and told him what had happened. That way I didn't have to tell him face to face. I was too ashamed by my own carelessness to tell someone to their face what I'd done.

I went home, got changed, went back to the hospital, and received some heartening news. Nathan did not have concussion, he had no broken bones, and there was no sign of water into his lungs.

They were wrong about that last part. He had inhaled a small amount of river water. The tide was going out when we'd had our accident, and it was carrying mud, weed and the kinds of gunk you'd expect to find in the water of a fishing port. Nathan might not have gotten much water in his lungs, but the little bit that he did inhale had some nasties in it. And they were festering away in his lungs even as I was being reassured that everything was alright.

I stayed in Nathan's room until about ten that night. When I went home, I used my neighbour's mobile to call Val's brother Stephen. I told him what had happened. He offered to call Val in the US and let her know.

'Thanks, Steve,' I said, 'I'd appreciate that. And please reassure her that he's not in any danger.'

Not in any danger. Right!

'Tell her if she wants to call me, she can reach me on this number.'

I went to bed still angry at myself, but I wasn't worried; my boy was doing okay. I didn't sleep very well though.

At four in the morning the phone rang. It was Val.

'What have you done to my son?' There was the tension of a

worried mother in her voice.

Explaining what had happened, that I had not been watching where I was going, that I had put a wheel of Nathan's buggy over the edge of the path, that Nathan had fallen out of the buggy down three metres of rock and into the river, was one of the more difficult things I have ever had to do. I expected Val to go off her head at me. I felt that that was what I deserved. She didn't. Once she found that Nathan was alright – although that, under the circumstances, was a little different from our normal interpretation of what is or is not alright – she was calm and measured. She even went out of her way to reassure me that it was an accident, that accidents happen, and that I shouldn't beat myself up over it.

I asked her to forgive me, but she said there was nothing to forgive. We said all the I-love-you-things and hung up.

When I went back to the hospital the next morning, the nursing staff told me that Nathan had had a good night, that he was doing well, and that I could take him home. He was sleeping when we left the hospital, and I was positive about life, myself, and Nathan's wellbeing. But, on the way back to Ballarat, my equanimity was getting a bit rattled. Nathan was still sleeping, but he was breathing heavily, in short, shallow gasps, and he was looking quite flushed. Another problem was that he hadn't peed for quite a few hours. That was usually a sign that he' wasn't well.

I got him home and he still hadn't woken, still hadn't peed. He was breathing like he'd run a 400-metre race.

I called the hospital and gave the nurse a rundown of the accident, Nathan's disability, and his symptoms. She didn't seem overly concerned, but she said I should bring him in just in case.

In the hospital parking lot, as I was lifting Nathan out of the car and into the wheelchair, I saw that he had peed so heavily that it had soaked through his diaper and wet his pants. I thought it was a bit of a nuisance, but I was relieved that he'd finally opened his bladder. His not peeing was one of the reasons I was taking him into emergency. Now that he had peed, I considered loading him back into the car and going home. I thought about it. I nearly did it. Thank God I didn't.

When I got into Emergency and told the intern about the disability, the accident, and the symptoms, she took one look at Nathan then must have hit a button that I didn't see. All of a sudden, there were people coming from everywhere. A swarm of nurses, doctors and interns took Nathan's blood pressure, temperature, oxygen saturation levels and pulse rate. They leaned over him and looked, prodded, searched, and discussed what they were seeing in hushed tones.

Then one of them took me aside and sat me down. He looked me in the eye and he said, 'Your son has pulmonary pneumonia. He's facing a pretty tough battle over the next few hours.'

Early in Nathan's life, when we were trying to learn about his disability and all that it meant, we were told that the biggest threat to Nathan's life would be a chest infection. Now he had a bad one. And I'd given it to him.

'What are his chances?' I asked.

'It depends,' said the doctor. That was not what I was hoping he'd say.

'What does it depend on?'

'It depends on whether or not he's a fighter. If he is, he's got a chance. At the moment though, he's hanging on by a thread.'

My God! What had I done to my son?

They took Nathan up to Intensive Care. I sat next to him and watched him. The hours ticked by. I wondered briefly how many times Nathan had been in an IC ward. When the IC staff finally realised I wasn't going to go home they gave me a fold-away bed in his room. I lay down and fixed my eye on Nathan, determined that I was going to watch him through the night. But, in spite of my good intentions, I went straight off to sleep. Sometime during the night, I woke just enough to realise that there was a small knot of medical staff bending over Nathan and working on him. They reassured me that he was doing as well as could be expected. I drifted back to sleep.

I woke at 5 a.m., kept vigil for a few hours, then went home to shower and change.

It was a 20-minute drive from the hospital to my place. I think my eyes were dry for maybe one of those 20 minutes. I was

134

trying to take in the possibility that I might have killed my son.

There were two really bad moments in all of this. The first one was when I was told that Nathan had pneumonia. The second one was when I called Val.

After she had completed her business dealings, she had taken some holiday time. She was staying at her sister's place in Oregon. She was due to take a flight home three days after I made this call.

Her sister Janet answered the phone. I cut through all the small talk and asked to speak to Val.

'Hi hon,' Val said. There was a lightness in her voice. She must have been having a nice time.

'Nathan is in Intensive Care in hospital,' I said. 'He has pulmonary pneumonia. He inhaled some organisms into his lungs when he fell into the river.'

Val is a strong woman, but when she asked the next question there was a tremor in her voice that I knew was caused by fear. 'Is he going to die?'

How do you answer that question? It was the same as, 'Have you killed him?'

'I don't know,' I said. 'He's battling hard, but…' then I fell apart again.

I have no doubt that Val's part in all of this was very hard. She spent the next few hours trying to arrange an early flight home. She called me for an update every hour. There wasn't much I could tell her. When she got on the plane for the flight to Australia she still didn't know if Nathan was going to make it. She sat on the plane, not knowing, for 18 hours.

Eighteen hours, with no news. Eighteen hours in which she didn't know if her only child was alive or dead.

When I got back into Nathan's room in the hospital, he rewarded me with a dazzling smile. My heart lifted: he was feeling better, he was going to be okay.

But the smile was because he was glad to see me, not because he was out of danger. In fact, he was heading into the toughest fight of his young life. For 48 hours, he was on a shadow-line between life and death.

A few hours later, Nathan's paediatrician (his name was Harry, and he knew Nathan well) brought a group of interns into Nathan's room on rounds. He asked me to tell his group what had happened. Bluntly, with no disguising of my part in the whole affair, I said I'd been careless, that I'd put a wheel of his buggy over the edge of a walk near the river in Port Fairy, that Nathan had inhaled some water, that he'd got pneumonia, and that he only had one lung. What else could I say?

The day dragged by in grey and listless seconds. I sat by Nathan's bed and watched my son fight. How long, I wondered could he keep gasping and panting like that? Occasionally, he looked like he was rallying. His pulse rate would drop below a 150, his breathing would ease a little, and once or twice his eyelids fluttered open. But the nurse said that these things happened because of the drugs he'd been given, and that there was no sign of a change in his condition.

The paediatrician came back. His name was Harry. 'We're thinking of putting him in an ambulance and sending him down to the Children's hospital', he said. 'They're much better equipped to deal with a severe case like this, and it may be Nathan's only chance.'

The last two words weighed on me like a ton.

'If it's his only chance, why are we just *thinking* about it?' I asked.

'He'll have to be put on a respirator,' said Harry.

'So?'

'There's a risk, with cerebral palsy kids, that if you put them on a respirator their lungs start to rely on it and you can never take them off.'

I felt like I was living a nightmare. Only there was no waking from this, and it was getting worse and worse.

'We're going to have to make a decision soon,' said Harry, 'but we'll wait a little while and see how he goes.'

I leant over my son. 'You keep fighting,' I told him. 'You fight until we're through this.'

'No,' said Harry, 'he may get too tired to keep fighting. And if he does, it's alright for him to stop.'

I had known Harry for most of Nathan's 18 years on this planet. I liked him, and most of the time I respected his judgement. But at that moment I so, so disagreed with him.

When he left the room, I turned back to Nathan. 'You keep fighting,' I said. 'You keep fighting until you win.' I didn't realise I was crying until the nurse handed me a box of tissues.

Sometime deep in the night, my brother Roger arrived. As he had done when Nathan was born, he had driven from Sydney as soon as he heard that Nathan was in trouble. My other two brothers would have been there if they were able, but Noel had surgeries scheduled, and Paul was up in Nimbin and too far away.

Not long after Roger arrived, Val's brother Steve and his family came up from Melbourne. As with Roger, there wasn't much for them to do, but they wanted to be there, and I needed the support.

Harry came back some time in the morning. He took me into the visitors lounge and asked me to sit me down. This was ominous. I sat. Fear clutched at my gut with an iron grip.

Harry sat down beside me. He sighed, and looked at the floor. 'We need to make a decision,' he said. 'Either we put him on a respirator and send him to Melbourne, or we continue treatment here.'

'I need your help here, Harry,' I said. 'I'm scared to death of Nathan going onto a respirator, but you're the expert, and if you say his best chance is in going to Melbourne…'

'That's his best chance,' said Harry.

There was a lump in my throat big enough to choke me. I tried to speak but I couldn't get the words out.

'Robin,' said Harry, 'this is hard, very hard. But I think we need to send him to Melbourne. They can do things for him there we can't do here.'

I nodded. The tears were spilling down my face. I didn't care.

Harry went to call the Children's Hospital to tell them that Nathan was coming. He was advised to fit Nathan with an oxygen mask that clamped hard over his mouth and forced air into his lungs, in a way that would keep them opened and distended. This would help him to breathe, and breathing was Nathan's hardest chore.

I went back to Nathan's bedside. I sat there with Roger and Steve. We watched Nathan, and we watched the monitors. We did that for the rest of the day.

Nathan's breathing rasped so loud he sounded like a smoker trying to run a marathon.

Evening came. The medical staff started preparations to take Nathan to Melbourne. But his condition wasn't worsening, so his departure was put off until the next morning.

Fatigue, from stress and from lack of sleep due to stress, was getting the better of me. I wanted to stay awake and watch, but Steve and Roger convinced me to take a break. I laid down on a fold-out bed beside Nathan and slept. Every now and then I woke up, but even as I went to get up and check on my son a woolly cloud of sleep pulled down over my head, and I was asleep again before my head hit the pillow.

I woke at six with a start. I jumped up and checked Nathan. He was still alive. I looked at his monitors. His pulse rate was down a little, and his breathing had eased just a fraction.

'He's holding his own,' said the nurse. 'We've postponed sending him to Melbourne.'

And just like that, he had turned the corner. He was going to live.

That afternoon, Roger brought his guitar into Nathan's room. He's a good guitarist. He played, and some of the IC staff gathered outside Nathan's room to listen. The liquid sound of fingers on strings filled the air, and the medical staff smiled and nodded their heads to the beat of the music. I felt as full of life as I had ever felt.

My boy was alive.

He had fought. And he had won.

If you could sole your boots with this kid's guts, they'd last you for life.
– Alan Marshall, *I Can Jump Puddles*

Chapter 15: Skiing

When Nathan was ten, we told our friends we were taking him skiing. Some of them rolled their eyes and stayed silent, their thoughts, *they have got to be crazy*, hanging like neon bubbles over their heads. Others stared at us in wonder and said nice things about what good parents we were. We liked that. It's bullshit though to think that taking your boy on an adventure holiday is an indication of good parenting.

Like so many things in our lives, the decision to go skiing was a little complicated. Skiing is a lot of fun, but, for us, taking Nathan skiing was something more. Just getting to Falls Creek was a challenge. Getting Nathan out onto the slopes, well... more than a few people told us it couldn't be done.

We had taken him skiing a few years back, when he was smaller and easier to lift and carry. It worked out fine. He seemed to have as much fun as we did.

As always when we organised a holiday with Nathan, Val spent a long-time planning. By the time we headed for Falls Creek, she had booked his sit-ski, and an instructor called Davie who was to manage the sit-ski and arranged for a carer to look after Nathan while we were out on the slopes.

We booked into the Falls Creek Country Club. Sounds fancy but it was just another ski lodge, with the advantage of being well placed for getting Nathan up to the ski lifts. Still, to get him to the ski lifts involved six lifts.

Got Nathan out of the wheelchair onto the bed to get him into his ski clothes.

Off the bed back into his wheelchair. Now he was about five kilos heavier because of the ski clothes.

Down to the car – a four-wheel-drive, not a car with wheelchair access. Lifted him out of the chair into the car. Packed the wheelchair into the car, drove about 200 meters and parked as close as we could to the ski lifts. Put the chair back together and lifted Nathan back into it. Pushed the chair closer to the snow – there was no way we could push his chair onto the snow – to a place where Davie the instructor would be waiting with the sit-ski.

Lifted Nathan out of his chair and, with Davie's help, lowered him into the sit-ski.

After this, I needed a rest. And there was still skiing to do. And then the four lifts at the end of the session that were needed to get Nathan back into our rooms at the Country Club. By the end of the day, I was well and truly buggered.

The last time we went skiing it was a big family affair and we had lots of family to help with the lifting and carrying. This time, there was my mate Nick and his wife Christine. Not as much help as last time, but it was enough.

On the first day the ski conditions were good – lots of fresh snow. I'm not a good skier, and with rusty skills, a bad knee and the determination to beat Nick down the slope every time, by the time I got through a few runs I was pretty tired.

By afternoon, it was time to take Nathan for his first run. When he was lowered into the sit-ski and strapped securely into place, he started to get a little worried. His face had that familiar *what are you guys doing to me?* look. Davie pushed him up to the ski lift, cranked the chair of the sit-ski a little higher, and the chair of the ski lift slid in underneath and they were away. Nathan was riding his sit-ski in the chairlift with Davie at his side. At the top, the lift slowed, and Nathan skied off the lift with Davie guiding him with the handles that jut out the back of the sit-ski. He was at the top of the hill and ready for his first run.

As he started down the hill, he was a little startled. He'd done it before, but who knows how adequate his memory was. A hundred metres down the hill he started to smile, and the further we got down the hill the bigger his smile got. By the time we reached the bottom, he looked like his face might split in two.

'Do you think he's enjoying it?' Davie asked.

'No doubt about it,' said Val.

On the second run, Davie pulled up halfway down the slope. He turned to Val. 'Do you want to steer Nathan for a little bit?' I tried not to let my pride be wounded because he didn't ask me.

Val hesitated. 'Umm, err, I...'

'C'mon,' said Davie. 'It's easy. I'll teach you. Here, take hold of the handles.'

Val was still uncertain, but once she was moving towards the sit-ski she was committed. She passed me her ski poles and grasped the handles at the back of the sit-ski.

'If you want to turn left, just turn the handles that way,' said Davie. 'It's just like riding a bike. When you turn the handles to the left, the skis edge onto the left side, so you turn left. And when you start moving, you control your speed by snow ploughing your own skis.'

Val and Nathan started moving, a slow and tentative glide. They curved left, picked up a little speed, curved right, rode gently over some moguls then stopped. They'd covered about 200 metres.

'You take over,' Val said to Davie. 'My legs are turning to jelly.'

'Oh, yeah,' said Davie, 'I forgot to mention, it's hard on the legs.'

On most days of this holiday the weather was perfect. I skied with Val or Nick in the mornings, and I beat Nick down the hill on every single run. In the afternoons I skied with Val and Nathan and Davie. It was proving to be a great holiday. The only problem was that, with skiing, lifting and carrying, I was becoming increasingly tired.

We reached day four without any incidents. The skiing again was good. We got more runs in than on previous days as we knocked the rust spots off our skills, but by evening I was really feeling the fatigue.

Back at the lodge, I lifted Nathan out of the car and put him in his chair. As we took the lift up to our room, I leaned back against the elevator wall and told Val I was so knackered I needed to go to bed early. We exited the lift, I pushed Nathan down the hallway and knocked on our door. Nick opened it, and I started to push Nathan inside. But there was a single step, down, just inside the door, and, because I was tired, I didn't hold onto Nate's wheelchair properly.

Earlier in this story I said that when you care for a Nathan it requires constant vigilance. And then I related a story about what happened when my vigilance lapsed. This was another of those times, but this time it wasn't just the momentary lapse in attention that caused the problem. When I'd taken him out of the car and put him in his wheelchair, I didn't buckle him in.

Stupid. Careless.

I can perhaps say I was tired, but fatigue doesn't mean I have less responsibility for Nathan's welfare. When his front wheels went over the step, I was holding onto the handles with the grip of a tired man. The wheelchair lurched forward, I lost my grip on the handles and Nathan was spat out from the front of the wheelchair like a stone from a slingshot. His face hit the carpet, which was coarse, industrial stuff – the kind of carpet you'd lay when people are going to walk on it in ski boots. He hit the carpet and skidded to a stop.

Now here's the moment – just a moment – when I didn't react well.

I could see the blood spilling from Nathan's face into the carpet. He let out a wail that could break your heart. I hurled the car keys that I was holding onto the floor – make no mistake, I hurled them, your classic tired-and-pissed-off dummy spit – and lunged for my boy. Nick helped me to get Nathan off the floor and into his wheelchair. Then we examined the damage.

There didn't seem to be much, just a bit of blood and some ugly carpet burns on his forehead that were probably stinging like crazy. The real damage though was to the car keys. There was a remote on them for locking and unlocking the car, and because I threw them when Nathan hit the floor, the remote was toast.

To get the car started again we needed a new remote. We called the closest Nissan dealer, in Wangaratta. We were told we'd have to have the car towed to Wangaratta, 140 winding kms away, so a new remote could be adapted to our car's computer system.

We looked for a cheaper way. We called the RACV. The mechanic had to come from Beechworth. He got to Falls Creek at ten that night, but because the car had its computer shut down when the car was locked, he couldn't do anything.

We ended up calling our friend Wendy in Ballarat. She had to go out to our place, get remote, and have it couriered up to Falls Creek.

One of the things Nathan helped me to learn: dummy spits are counter-productive.

Chapter 16: Sabah

'Rob!'

Val's voice cuts through the fog of sleep. I try to ignore it.

'Rob!' Sharp and demanding. Knuckles dig into my ribs. 'Rob, I'm worried that we didn't get malaria shots.'

'What time is it? Two a.m.? For chrissake, go back to sleep.'

'But I'm worried. What if we get bitten by mosquitoes? We might get malaria'

I'm awake now, and irritated. 'Val, we're not going to get bitten by mosquitoes carrying malaria bugs. We're staying at a resort. Go to sleep.'

Five minutes later a gentle snore tells me she's gone. Me, I'm wide awake. I don't mind though. I've got something to think about, and it's not the possibility of contracting malaria. We're taking our boy to Borneo. We leave in three days, which is soon enough for me to savour the anticipation, and soon enough for Val to turn her into a nervous wreck. She, after all, is the planner. My job is to tote and carry. Nathan's job is to be Nathan. Neither his or my job involves worrying.

We have learnt from our Costa Rica, skiing and Port Fairy trips that even with careful planning things can go wrong. Still, I'm not worrying. I never anticipate things going wrong – I'm the eternal optimist. I reckon I could get Nathan to Paris in a Tiger Moth if I had to. Val is the worrier. Val, of course, is determined that nothing will go wrong, so she's planning for every possibility – bar malaria. We've had flu shots, Hep A booster shots, tetanus shots. We've bought a portable nebuliser. We've had a moulded seat back made for Nathan to use on the plane or when he's sitting in a banana seat by the resort pool.

Val drove to the airport a month before we left to pick up a bike box for Nathan's beach buggy. She was pissed off when she did it, because I hadn't gone. I wanted to wait until we drove to the airport to fly out and buy the box then. That's the difference between us.

Two days to go. The bags are already packed. Val takes two small syringes out of the medicine cabinet and fills them with glycerine. She pulls on a pair of plastic gloves, lies Nathan on the bed and squirts a shot of glycerine up his bum. He needs to empty his bowels before we go, so he doesn't do it while we're on the plane.

One day to go. Unreasonable demands are made as Val's stress levels climb ever higher. It doesn't stop Nathan and me from getting more and more excited. I do my best to accommodate her unreasonable demands.

D-Day. Packing the car isn't a problem this time because we're taking two cars. Jane, again, is coming to the airport with us, and some of the luggage goes in her car.

The trip to the airport, unloading, getting to the check-in counter, all happens without any drama. The check-in clerk is polite and friendly, but he tells us all the bulkhead seats, which we ask for because they're easier to get Nathan in and out of, are already booked.

'Babies in cribs get priority,' he says. 'The closest to the door I can give you is Row 22. It's quite close to the door.'

A pain, I guess, but we can manage it. At least there's none of the *you-have-to-use-an-aisle-wheelchair* bullshit.

We go to the bar for our standard celebratory drink. Memories of the Costa Rica trip, Nathan's chest infection, perfectly timed to be at the worst possible moment, lurk in our minds. Nathan coughs, just a little one, and we all jump, stare, hold our collective breath.

He grins his big infectious grin. His way of saying, 'Tricked ya!'

When we're called to board, and I get to the part where I have to lift Nathan out of his wheelchair and carry him to his seat, I find that the aisles are narrower and the seat-backs higher than on other airlines we've flown with. And Row 22, after getting through first class and business class, is a long way from the door.

With a little grunting and panting I get Nathan into place. We settle down, everybody else boards. As we get ready for take-off, I'm peeved to see that the bulkhead seats are all taken by strapping young adults. Not a baby crib in sight.

It's eight uneventful hours to Kuala Lumpur, except we're very late touching down. We have to change planes, and, because of our next flight leaving soon, plus waiting, waiting, waiting for the wheelchair to come, we get a bit stressed. No problems, though: we get there with all of 30 seconds to spare.

Kuala Lumpur to Kota Kinabalu is just two hours. Nathan's bowels behave, and his condom holds up. Ah, holidays. It's going to be a good two weeks.

At Kota Kinabalu we get our bags and the bike box off the carousel, stack it onto three luggage carriers and start wending our way through the crowds towards the exit. A Customs guy comes running over to us, takes one of the carriers, calls to one of his staff who takes another one, and the five of us and three mounds of baggage head out of the airport.

Outside it is hot and humid. Worse than humid, it's steamy. A driver is there waving a sign that says Runyan, so the promise of car air-conditioning is tantalisingly close. He takes us to his vehicle, then we say thank-you and goodbye to the friendly customs men and open up the car to start packing the wheelchair, running buggy and bags. We find we've got a six-seater car, where the back two seats fold away but take up a lot of room, and there's not much packing space. Nathan goes into the front passenger seat, his wheelchair gets taken apart, and chair, cases and bike box are packed, unpacked, repacked. The only way we can get it all in is if Val and I share one seat and put two of the smaller cases on our laps. We head out into peak hour traffic for one of the slowest and most cramped trips I've ever had. At least the air-conditioning works.

Our first impressions of Kota Kinabalu aren't all that positive. It seems dirty and ramshackle, and we get to examine it fairly well because we stand in traffic jams for long periods. But eventually the traffic thins, and suburbs of cement and cast-iron give way to villages, jungle, swamps and rivers.

We pull into the resort, and the place looks immaculate. The formalities of check-in are quickly out of the way and we're taken to our room. Val, who has been so calm and collected, is now like a kid in a candy store who wants to eat everything at once. She wants to sit on the terrace outside our room, hang out in the bar in the foyer, go swimming in the pool, lie on the beach. And she wants to do it all at once. She wants to hit the top speed of relaxing as quickly as possible. Nathan, being the seasoned traveller that he is, takes everything in his stride.

We leave the room and explore the resort. The hotel staff fuss over Nathan like he's royalty. He soaks it up, smiling so big it could bust his face.

In the late afternoon we go back to our room, get Nathan into his running buggy and have a couple of gin and tonics to fortify ourselves for our first evening at Rasa Ria. The trouble is that I'm not an experienced spirits man, and gin tastes so mild. I mix the drinks so they're close to 50% gin, and they slide down easily. Time to hit the beach.

The sand at Rasa Ria is white and super fine. The beach is wide. It requires some real shoving, grunting and sweating to push boy and buggy across some 70 metres of powdery sand. By the time we get to the water's edge I'm knackered. On the firmer sand close to the water, Val takes Nathan, I lie down, the world spins, and I realise that I'm very drunk. Hell, doesn't matter, I'm on holiday. I close my eyes and begin a gentle slide into the first snooze of my vacation. Then...

'Rob, get up,' a voice blurts. 'I can't push Nathan another step. Y'know, you made those G & Ts way too strong.'

I am dragged off the sand and harnessed behind the buggy for pushing duties.

'I'm drunk,' I say.

'Me too,' says Val. 'It's just as well Nathan's driving – he's the only one of us that's sober.' We both start giggling.

By now the alcohol is well and truly working its wicked magic. As we lumber back across the sand, towards the beach bar and substances to buttress our drunken state, I push Nathan, Val pushes me – it's been too long since she's put her hands on my butt – instead of helping to push the buggy. Our giggling has changed to helpless laughter, and we stop several times to catch our breath. It must look odd, this little line of three struggling across the sand. Eventually, one of the drinkers at the beach bar detaches himself from the throng and comes across the beach towards us.

'Do ye need help,' he asks, in a heavy Scottish accent, 'or are ye jest havin' a good time?'

We collapse in gales of laughter, though what he said wasn't that funny, and Val finally gasps out that, yes, some help would be appreciated. He takes the front wheel, I push Nate, Val pushes me, and we make it to the oasis where more drinks are available. We buy one for our helper.

The rest of the evening is rather woolly in my memory. I do recall standing up with the band and singing along with them. I remember having an argument with Val because she wanted me to go back to the food table and get her some of what I had because it looked so good, and I wouldn't go because I couldn't remember which of several food tables I'd got it from. I remember Nathan chuckling and vocalising like he was drunk along with his parents. It wasn't until the next morning, when I got up and looked at my and Val's clothes from the night before, and saw how they were smeared with chocolate, that I remembered our attack on the fondue bar. That first day would have to be categorised as an outstanding success.

The pool is our main destination for the second day. In fact, the pool, which is large, blue, warm and crystal clear, will be the centre of our activities for most days at Rasa Ria. After breakfast, we go to stake out our poolside claim. There are parts of pool that slope down gently, from very shallow into deeper water. We want a place at the shallow end, because that's where we'll be getting Nathan in and out. The resort isn't that crowded, less than half full I'd guess, but most of the pool side chairs are taken. We call a lifeguard, and ask him if we can move some chairs so we're near the shallow entry.

He studies Nathan carefully. 'How old is he?' he asks.

'Nineteen.'

'Ah, same as me. What is his name?'

'Nathan.'

He takes Nathan's tightly clenched fist in his hand. 'Hello Nathan. My name is Ronnie. I will look after you when you come to the pool.'

Every morning after that, Ronny reserves us three seats, under a big umbrella, close to the shallow entry point.

Getting Nathan in and out of the chair is a well-established procedure. It's not difficult as long as my back holds up. I get my left arm behind his back, the right under his thighs. I position my feet carefully, keep my head up and by bum tucked in. One, two, three Lift, with a strong exhalation of breath. The lifting is the hardest part; carrying him the short distance into the pool is easy. Once the water reaches up past my knees I can sit down and let the water do most of the carrying.

Nathan loves being in the pool. The water is so warm it's easy to stay in there for a long time. On most days we stay in the pool until we're bored, though Val says she's gets out because her skin is getting wrinkled. When we get Nathan out of the pool, we drape a towel over a deck chair and put him there instead of his wheelchair.

We're in and out of the pool several times through the day. After the third time, as I'm carrying Nathan back to his deck chair, Val leans over the chair and sniffs.

'He's peed on the chair,' she says. 'It stinks.'

Before leaving the room, we'd taken Nate's condom, catheter and shield off. We thought he'd probably pee in the pool, but, apparently, he's absorbed all those home messages about not peeing in public pools. He has saved it until he comes out of the water, and he's peed in his trunks and onto the resort towel he's sitting on.

In the minds of humans there is some kind of a correlation between disability and that smell. For the parent, it's like an emblem of shame. We live in dread of some well-meaning person leaning over Nathan to greet him, and then recoiling in revulsion as the odour of urine hits their nose. We have images of them wanting to get away from our son, of them thinking of us as bad parents.

We need a different strategy for pool times. We leave his condom on, and take the catheter bag off when we go into the pool, and replace it when we get out and before he can pee on the towel.

***

One of our reasons for choosing the Rasa Ria Resort was that it had an orangutan sanctuary. Val had emailed and phoned the resort before we left Australia, explained Nathan's special needs and enquired about getting Nathan's wheelchair into the jungle, to the place where the orangutan viewing took place. She had been assured that it would be no problem.

On the second day, I go to the sanctuary and ask to be shown the track up which we would take Nathan in his running buggy to see the orangutans. Being a cock-eyed optimist, I'm confident my super powers will allow me to overcome obstacles like uneven terrain, steep grades, tree roots, and even a stair or two. Surely, if septuagenarians and unfit tourists can make it, I, my boy and our joint determination will make it too.

I am shown a narrow and winding trail. Tree roots and rocks make a rough surface even rougher, and there're a lot of steep and uneven stairs. There is no chance of taking Nathan up there.

I go back to the room and tell Val what I've found. Straight away she's onto the phone to talk to the rangers at the sanctuary.

'The reason we chose this resort,' she tells them, 'is because of the sanctuary, and because of your assurances that we could get Nathan in to the viewing points to see the orangutans.'

'Madam,' she is told, 'they are wild animals. We cannot make any promises, but we will see about arranging a private viewing for your son. We will try to bring one of the orangutans down to the edge of the jungle for him.'

The next day, at the appointed time, we head over to the sanctuary to see if the rangers can make good on their promise. The ranger at the reception desk explains again that they cannot promise that an orangutan will be there.

'Exactly where?' asks Val.

The ranger waves her hand in the general direction of the

jungle. 'Not far. Just into the forest a little.'

'Will there by mosquitoes?'

'Oh yes,' says the ranger. 'Many, many mosquitoes.

We spend the next ten minutes lathering ourselves with insect repellent. Nathan hates the smell. He wrinkles his nose and screws up his mouth like he's tasting something nasty, though we take care he doesn't get any in his mouth. We can't understand why a group of rangers sitting at a table in the reception centre is laughing at us.

A ranger comes in from outside and signals for us to follow him. He heads for the track I saw yesterday, the one that blasted my hopes of being able to take Nathan up to the orangutan viewing station.

'How far do we have to go?' I ask, and I wave my hand towards Nathan and Val, to explain the impossibility of getting Nathan up the track. But before I can say anything, the Ranger points.

Twenty metres along the track – and, by the way, there is not a mosquito in sight – there's another ranger, and an orangutan clinging shyly to his leg. As we get closer, the orangutan buries his face in the cloth of the ranger's pants, and peeks at us as though we're something dangerous. His name is Reggie. I hesitate to use the word, but he is so damned cute. Human-like. Apparently, an orangutan's DNA is 96% identical to that of a human's.

Nathan is clearly intrigued. He has trouble focussing his eyes on things, but he is trying his best to focus on Reggie, who, after he gets over seeing us as a threat, is equally interested in Nathan. From the safety of the ranger's shoulder, he reaches out a long and slender arm towards Nathan, but the ranger intercepts the enquiring hand. There is to be no contact between Reggie and any of us. Reggie peers over the ranger's shoulder at Nathan, then changes position and looks at him again from a different angle. He keeps watching Nathan the whole time until we leave. He does not look at Val or me at all.

We leave the sanctuary, and Val and I talk about why Reggie was interested in Nathan but not in us. It seems that he could tell that Nathan was different from the other humans he'd encountered.

On the walk back to our room, Nathan is vocalising like crazy, telling us over and over again his version of the meeting with Reggie. Is he really doing that? Is he talking about the strange red-brown creature that he just met? Is he talking about an orangutan called Reggie, or has he been stimulated by something we don't know about, something other than Reggie? Or is he just making noise? We don't really know. A career as a researcher has taught me that the occurrence of two variables together (variable 1 = Nathan meets Reggie; variable 2 = Nathan is excited) is not evidence that the two variables are linked. But we want to believe that in this case they are. And we are pleased.

***

There's not much difference between the fourth day, the fifth and the sixth. Nathan is getting to be known around the resort – it's hard to miss a kid in a wheelchair – and strangers say hello to him.

We decide it's time to get out of the resort, and we book dinner at a seafood restaurant not far away.

The restaurant looks like a bit of a dive, but not much effort is made with décor in Asia once you get away from the tourist places. It's large, open-aired and built on the edge of a mangrove swamp. When the tide is high it would be as pretty as a picture, but we arrive when the tide is way out, and the view is over mud flats that have a distinctive odour. Still, to us, it's all new and different. At least it's easy to get Nathan in and around.

We have to make our menu selection from tanks of live seafood.

'You pick,' says the hostess.

Cool. And we know it's going to be fresh. I order oysters natural and king prawns. Val orders lobster.

'Don't you think it's a bit risky ordering raw oysters?' she asks.

'They're fresh. We saw them in the tank, still in water, with their shells closed,' I reply. I can be so stupid sometimes.

I'm a bit confused when the hostess directs my attention to a cardboard plate, with a pea, a mushroom, and several different

152

pieces of greenery on it.

You pick,' says the hostess. I think those are her only words of English.

I point at the mushroom and a strange piece of green stuff.

The food is terrific. The oysters are fresh, cold, coated in ice, the prawns are spicy and the lobster is as tender as butter. A good night is had by all. Nathan stays alert until we catch the cab home, and all the way back to the resort he tells the driver about his night.

***

Taking Nathan to a country like Malaysia, where the disabled are not part of the wider community and no arrangements are made for their inclusion, was, from the time we started planning the trip, a bit of a gamble. But we told ourselves that we managed Costa Rica okay, and Fiji, so there was no reason why we couldn't do Borneo.

Now, for a family with a highly dependent kid, such a trip is doable, but the doability depends on three things.

First, the planning has to be detailed and flawless. And I had Val, one of the world's premier planners. No problems there.

Second, the trip's success depends on the cooperation of the people we deal with along the way. This is always a bit of an unknown. I learnt in an Introduction to Logic class that, just because an object thrown from a window falls to earth every time, it doesn't mean that it will fall to earth the next time. And, following that line of logic, we cannot assume that, because people have been incredibly kind and helpful in the past, they will be the next time we go travelling. Still, on our trips to Fiji, Costa Rica, Falls Creek, Nimbin, and even just down the road to Melbourne, we found that people saw Nathan, and their first thought was, how can I help? So, in spite of what my Logic lecturer said, the help of strangers, with a kid like Nathan, was a pretty sure bet.

Third, on any trip, short, long, complex or simple, attention to Nathan, particularly if he is on the move, has got to be constant. Things could go wrong, and they are more likely to go wrong if we were not paying very close attention to every detail. This lesson was hard learnt in the past.

Fourth, the doability of travelling with Nathan depended on my well-being. I had to do the grunt work: lift Nathan into and out of his wheelchair, the car, the plane seat, the shower, the pool. At home, I had a good exercise program and saw a chiropractor regularly to ensure I maintained my lifting capability.

***

After a few days at Rasa Ria, I count that I'm lifting him into or out of his chair 15-20 times a day. He weighs 55 kilos, but as long as I'm whole and healthy, on the fourth issue, no problems.

On the seventh day, I wake up with a tight and painful lower back. As far as bad backs go, it's not a bad one, but I know that picking Nathan up 15-20 times a day is going to aggravate it. I go to the gym and do some careful and comprehensive stretching. It doesn't help. I finish my program and my back is still clenched like a steel fist. When I look in the mirror, the twist in my lower torso is obvious.

I book a massage for the afternoon. I manage to get Nathan in and out of the pool a couple of times, then I head to the spa centre for a massage.

When I come out, my back is still tight, and I'm feeling weird, spaced out. 'Must be the massage,' I tell myself. But as I get closer to the room, I can tell that it's more than that.

Just as I get to the room the oysters from last night – or the ice that covered them – come at me with a vengeance. Gastro. I start puking, and I can't stop. Then I get diarrhoea, and after an hour of puking and shitting I'm dehydrated. One minute I'm shivering and the next I'm drenched in sweat. My stomach is cramping every couple of minutes. When it happens, I feel like my gut is in a vice. I whimper. Tough, manly resilient me, whimpering like a baby.

The fourth point of doability is now a definite problem. Poor Val is having visions of me in hospital, and her with a disabled boy she cannot lift. Her stress is obvious, even to me in the state I'm in, when she yells at me to stop when I'm dry-retching in the bathroom.

I'm suffering enough for Val to call a doctor. While she's waiting for him to come, she manages to get Nathan out of the wheelchair and onto the bed. Undoubtedly, if she needs to, she'll be able to get him back into it, but getting him into the pool or the bath will be beyond her.

It comes as no surprise when the doctor tells us I'm suffering an acute bout of gastroenteritis. He gives me a number of drugs and tells me he'll call in again tomorrow.

The next morning, I feel like death, but at least I'm not vomiting or shivering. The stomach pains have eased; they still hit, but less frequently. Ditto the diarrhoea. Nathan and I spend the day in the room, while Val takes a taxi to do the tourist thing in Kota Kinabalu.

The next day we're back at the pool. I am surprised at how much the gastro has drained my strength. With the loss of strength and my sore back it is much harder to lift Nathan. The lustre goes from our holiday.

***

Enough with the details. Suffice to say that taking a boy like Nathan on a holiday is doable, but it depends – besides the above four points – on everything going to plan. Getting everything to go accordingly depends on just how carefully you lay those plans, though there is something said by sages about plans, mice and men.

Chapter 17: The Concert

Usually, Saturday is a rest day for me, but this morning I had to make a presentation to a sporting group at work. I straightened my tie and listened to Val talking to Nathan in the kitchen. As she was telling him what was in the morning paper and asking him what he wanted to do for his birthday, I put on my jacket and reached for my briefcase.

'Rob,' from the kitchen. Then a little louder. 'Rob.'

I heard, but I didn't answer. I was running through my presentation, well-rehearsed already, but to be presented within the hour.

'Rob.' This time with some urgency. I went into the kitchen to find out what she had to say. She had her finger on an ad in the paper and I saw she was excited.

'Look at this,' she said. 'We can make an early booking for the Rolling Stones. It would be a great birthday present for Nathan, don't you think?'

I'm not a big concert goer, but Nathan was hard to buy for – after all, he had everything – and the noise and buzz of a big concert would be a kick for him.

'Sounds like a great idea,' I said.

She reached for the phone, and I went back to running my presentation through my head. I had just reached the point where I would be explaining some research findings to my audience when I heard Val's voice go up a couple of octaves. I tuned in to what she was saying.

'You can't do that.' She sounded angry. I listened closer. 'You can't stop a person from booking just because they're in a wheelchair, when everyone else is able to book.'

Something was said by the booking operator on the other end of the line.

'I don't care if it's policy,' Val retorted. 'It's illegal. It's discrimination.'

There was a lengthy response from the booking operator, to which Val responded, 'Can I speak to your supervisor?'

I whispered to Val that I had to leave. She was so focussed on her phone conversation that I don't think she heard me. As I walked out the door, I thought to myself, *you guys should give up now. You haven't got a chance.*

My presentation went smoothly, and two hours later I was turning back into the drive of our house. As I pulled up, Val shot out of the house and pranced around my car chortling with glee.

'Front row tickets,' she crowed. 'We've got front row tickets to the Rolling Stones.'

'Wow! What... how...'

'I kept going up the ladder. When I went to book three tickets, they said okay, but when I said one of the three was in a wheelchair they said I couldn't book for him until Wednesday. I said that was illegal, and when I got stuck with one person I demanded to talk to their supervisor. I went through three people before the fourth one said she'd call me back. She called back an hour later to say, 'You're right, we're going to change our ticketing policy, and for your trouble would you like front row seats?'

'Front row seats!' Val said, dancing around like an excited school girl. 'Oh,' she added. 'and we've got free parking too.'

***

On the evening of the concert, we arrived at the venue a little late, partly because we were able to because we had a reserved parking spot, and partly because it's hard to time things precisely with Nathan. There's always some last little detail that puts us behind time. We got into the venue in the break between the cover band finishing and the Stones appearing. When we entered the concert hall it was like a giant cave. Spotlights arched and curved across the roof and a muted, excited rumble from 10,000 people filled the air. Nathan's eyes went wide, his attention levels ratcheted up to maximum. This, he knew, was something special. We worked our way through the throng to the front of the auditorium.

Our seats were perfectly centred in the front row. If we'd gone into the stadium before the concert and asked for the best seats in the house, those were the seats we'd been given.

But there was a catch. Isn't there always?

In front of the front row of seats, there was a security barrier. An iron fence, about 60 millimetres from the seats themselves. And Nathan's wheelchair is 80 millimetres wide.

'No problem,' said the security guard, 'we'll just put him, right here.' He pointed to the space at the end of the row, where Nathan would have his view of half of the stage obscured by a huge speaker, which, when the Stones were cranking, would blast him out of his chair.

Val shook her head. 'Now, I'm asking you,' she said, in her most reasonable voice, 'If you were 16 years old, and you had seats in the middle of the front row, and someone said you had to sit at the side instead, where you could only see half the stage, would you agree?'

"I'm sorry,' said the security guard, 'but there's nothing I can do about it.'

I'd heard that one before. Val of course was not going to accept it.

'Can I speak to your supervisor?' she asked. Oh, I love that woman.

We slowly worked our way up the chain of command, with a knot of security folk of ever-increasing size having their input. Val would not be moved, and I added my support by nodding sternly every time she spoke.

Eventually, one of them, someone with authority said, 'Alright, we'll have to undo the security barrier.' And everyone in the knot nodded their assent. We only held the concert up by a few minutes, and we got to our front-row-at-the-centre seats.

Nathan loved the concert. He was bug-eyed and grinning from the first song. And it was made even better when, about a third of the way through the concert, Keith Richards beckoned a roadie over, gave him something, spoke into his ear and pointed in our general direction. A few minutes later, the roadie appeared in front of us, and handed Keith Richards' guitar pick to Nathan.

And also...

The bass guitarist, who was not a regular member of the Rolling Stones, threw his guitar pick out into the audience after every song. There was a mad scramble every time, and as the concert progressed the pack of fans waiting in front of him grew and grew. One time, he threw his pick and it fell short of the waiting throng and dropped into the space between seats and security fence, in an area where it had not been unbolted. A security guard picked up, walked over to Nathan and gave it to him.

My boy had VIP written all over him. But I wondered, would he have been given the two guitar picks if he'd been sitting in the seat at the end of the row?

One of the things Val helped me learn was, if you're not satisfied, ask to speak to the supervisor.

Chapter 18: In the End, There Was Light

By Nathan's twentieth year, we believed we had things running well. Nathan's package from state and federal governments was sufficient for his needs, and he was involved in a number of activities. His carers knew him well. They were a big part of his life because they would arrive at our house at 8:30 every weekday morning, and be with him until five o'clock. He got to know them, and we were easily able to tell which ones he liked and which ones he didn't.

We'd seen off the tough times. Our lives were running like a well-oiled machine. Then, three months before Nathan turned 21, we moved.

Val was offered a job on the Gold Coast, and we had to bid farewell to our tried and trusted carers, to our well-established programs and our tight circle of friends, and face the two difficulties that we always faced when we moved somewhere with Nathan: finding suitable programs, and bureaucratic inertia.

In Ballarat, we had dealt with these two difficulties long enough to have pretty much removed any negative impact from them on Nathan's life. When we moved, we had to go through it all again. We had to reinvent Nathan's program from the ground up. This was, not surprisingly, quite frustrating. There were lots of agencies in our new home, offering a wide variety of services for the disabled, but a lot of them turned out to be duds. The biggest problem was that an agency provided place, space and helpers where the disabled could go and do... well, we don't really know what they were supposed to do when they got there. Sit and look and listen I suppose. A number of times, we took Nathan to a program, and, while we were there, nobody approached him to ask a question about who he was, what he wanted to do, or he could do. So, unless the carer took the initiative and helped Nathan to choose an activity he liked – assuming there was any choice at all – he just sat there and did nothing.

Surely, it's the carer's responsibility, I hear you say.

No, it is not.

The carers were there to support Nathan in whatever activity he undertook. They were not there to direct his activity. Programs that did not provide this direction were, as far as we're concerned, inadequate. It was one of the main criteria we looked for when judging a program, and, if the program didn't measure up on those criteria, we assumed that there was not enough interest from the providers for us to believe they would have Nathan's best interests at heart.

What would you think if your kid went to an art class, got given paints and paper, but no direction on what or how to paint? Inadequate, right?

After extensive winnowing, we found some program providers that were better than what he had in Ballarat, and some that were not quite as good. But his program still had a long way to go.

The biggest problem though was, again, the bureaucrats. We needed their help because they were supposed to allocate Nathan's funding, which was State-based, and we had changed States. But help they did not give, though they gave promises aplenty.

'Yes,' they said, 'Nathan needs to be funded.'

They assured us he would be funded, but days turned into weeks which turned into months, and the funding was not allocated. We don't know why, perhaps they were just trying to save money. Bureaucracies, by their very nature, are unfeeling and unmoving things, and the bureaucrats that work within them are often the same. They promised us, but they didn't seem to care that the promises were not fulfilled.

Getting them to take action on Nathan's behalf reinforced all over again the necessity of a good advocate. This time, I didn't question Val's actions or interfere with her operations. I stood back and watched.

I lost track of the number of meetings we had – though I know Val documented them all – and the higher we went the more immovable the bureaucrats were. It culminated in a session with a high-level public servant, who, we were told, had a background in disability services and therefore should be sympathetic to our cause. We went into the meeting with high hopes. What we got was an unending stream of bureaucratic gobbledegook that was unhelpful, uninterpretable, and could only have been meant to fob us off. The only question to which we got a direct answer was, 'How has your day been?'

When we left the meeting, I was feeling angry. I asked Val why she hadn't challenged him when he covered us in bullshit.

'It's ammunition,' she said.

I looked at her perplexed.

'I need to get to the minister for disabilities,' she explained. 'The more rubbish they hand us, the more ammunition we have when we get to the politicians, and that's going to make it harder for them to put us off.'

But put us off they did. Again, and again. Not just the bureaucrats, the politicians as well. Val was sending a steady stream of letters to politicians on both sides of the divide, pleading for their help, asking for meetings so we could explain our problem in detail. All to no avail. The responses might all have come from the same pen. The words differed a little, but the substance was the same as what was given by the bureaucrats: streams of gobbledegook that was unhelpful, uninterpretable, and could only have been meant to fob us off.

Our original arrangement with the Victorian government was that it would fund Nathan for a year, and after that the Queensland government should have taken over. But as 2011 wound down, we were no closer to getting funding than we were at the start of the year. In January 2012, our package from Victoria was extended for another month, then again in February and again in March, and at that time we were told the funding would definitely, irrevocably finish at the end of April.

I don't want to tarnish all of the staff of Queensland Disability Services with the same brush. Through this period, most of them wanted to help, tried to help, offered advice that was contrary to the official line, and was therefore advice that was not in their best interests. But they were stymied by bureaucratic inertia and the strange, inexplicable unhelpfulness of a small number of politicians and higher-ranking public servants.

It did sometimes seem that this attitude of learned unhelpfulness was only skin-deep, because after meeting Nathan some of the bureaucrats we dealt with changed their mindset. This phenomenon was typified by a woman from Disability Services who called us up, asked for a meeting, and thereby stimulated our hopes that at last something would be done. However, in the early stages of the meeting all we heard was the, *I'm sorry but there is nothing that can be done about it* line that we had heard so many times before. But towards the end of the meeting, as the woman was parroting her line for the fiftieth time, Nathan started to vocalise. He was tense, tightening his little body into a semi-foetal position and vocalising with a loud and irritated tone while his face was screwed up as though he had a nasty taste in his mouth. The woman stopped what she was saying and asked, 'What's the matter with him? Is he all right?'

Val studied him for a moment, and said, 'No, he's not alright. He knows I'm upset, and he doesn't like what you're saying.'

To her credit, the woman was quite disturbed by Nathan's distress. Her attitude and her message changed. The meeting finished with her promising that she would personally take up the cause and fight as hard as he could to get Nathan his funding. But she called us a week later and told us that she was being stymied by her superiors. We believed that she had tried, because she actually sounded like she was crying as she delivered us the bad news.

What to do? Further meetings with Disability Services proved to be futile, and it looked like we were going to be forced into making an unwelcome decision. By now, we had found that the warm Queensland climate really suited Nathan. He was clearly healthier and happier than he had been in Victoria, but, if we stayed in Queensland, we would lose almost all his funding. If we returned to Victoria, his full package would be reinstated, but there would be a deterioration in his well-being. In the end, with no movement from the government and their promises still unfulfilled, it seemed we had no choice but to go back. We contacted the tenants in our house in Wattle Flat, and told them we were coming back. We contacted Nathan's Ballarat carers, and found they were all available and keen to renew the relationship. Then Val handed in her notice at the university.

Her boss was horrified. He offered for the university to pay for Nathan's package, but, as generous as that offer was, it would have tied Val to the university for a number of years, and, when she finished there, we would again have been without a package for Nate. So, she refused the offer. They negotiated, and finally agreed that Val would work from home (in Victoria), with extensive use of Skype, the internet and email, and would travel up to the Gold Coast for four days of every fortnight, and the university would cover her accommodation costs. We booked the movers, gave notice of our departure to the real estate agents, and it was all settled. We were going back.

A few mornings later, Val was sitting in bed having her morning coffee. She was uncommunicative, staring into space and deep in thought. Finally, she said, "I can't believe I didn't win. I always win.' And she got up, went to work, and resumed the fight for Nathan's funding. But this time, the first thing she did was contact a lawyer.

It took a lot of to-ing and fro-ing, but a few weeks later the government saw things our way. Nathan got a package that was, though not equal to what he had in Victoria, adequate to his needs. However, we saw it as an indictment on the Queensland government that we had to fight for what should have been offered. Fortunately for us, it was an election year, so Val contacted the relevant politicians, told them we were willing to go to the press, that we had a good-looking boy and a story that would capture attention because of the upcoming election. It cost time, effort, stress and money to win what was initially promised and should have been given when we first arrived in the state.

In carrying out the fight, we spoke to a number of families in similar situations to ours. What was pleasing was that we won, and Nathan was able to live where he and his family wanted to live. What was not pleasing was that there were – still are – many Queensland families in the same boat. Unlike so many people, we had the financial capacity to use the legal system.

But, still, in other realms, the fight goes on. Life with a severely disabled kid is like that.

Chapter 19: The Commonwealth Games

2018 was a big year for the Gold Coast. It was the year of the Commonwealth Games. They were held in early April, and the whole region was agog with excitement for months before the opening ceremony.

In late 2017, Nate, Val and I were pretty much sick of hearing about the Games, so when an item came on the ABC news I tuned out. Val, of course, did not. She listened. After a couple of minutes she said, 'I think Nathan should try out for that.'

'Yep,' I said, thinking all the while about how to get rid of the mould on the ceiling of the living room.

'He'd probably be the only wheelchair applicant,' she said.

'Yep,' I said, while wondering about the sagacity of spraying bleach indoors.

'Do you know what I'm talking about?' asked Val.

'Ahh…' Sprung! 'No, sorry, Honey, I was just…'

'I was talking about the Commonwealth Games.'

My interest level plummeted.

'About Nathan trying out for the opening ceremony.'

My interest level rose to a height never reached on the topic of the Commonwealth Games since they were held in Melbourne in 2006.

'What role would he be trying out for?' I asked. 'Do you think they'd even look at him?'

'Well, they were just saying that they were having trouble getting enough dancers. They said that you didn't have to be a good dancer, or athletic, they just want the numbers.'

Though usually content to let Val take the lead I'd still been an advocate for Nate being given every possible chance to try every possible experience. But, still, on this one, I was sceptical.

'Y'know,' I said, 'when they said you didn't have to be a good dancer, they didn't have the Nathans of the world in mind.'

'Nothing ventured nothing gained,' said Val. 'There's an online application form. We'll send it in and see what happens.'

'Right,' I said, thinking to myself that the world was not yet progressive enough to find a role for the likes of Nate in an event like the Commonwealth Games' opening ceremony.

How wrong I was.

Val sent the application form in and, much to our surprise, she got a call from the organizing committee asking for Nathan to come to an audition.

You would know by now that Val was never backward when it comes to pushing Nathan's cause, but even she was taken aback by this offer. 'I don't want to waste anyone's time on this,' she said to whoever it was on the other end of the line, 'but perhaps you don't know just how disabled Nathan is. He cannot speak. He can't get out of his wheelchair. He definitely can't dance. Maybe—'

But the caller interrupted with,' Oh yes, we know all about Nathan. We know about his disabilities, and we would really like him to audition.'

'How do you know about his disabilities?' Val asked.

'We googled him,' said the caller. 'We had no idea of what he's capable of, and we now know what he's capable of, what he's not capable of, and we'd like him to audition.'

When Val hung up the first thing she did was google Nathan's name to see what the ceremony organisers saw. She found the article from the Port Fairy newspaper, *The Moyne Gazette*, which covered Val's fight to get beach access for wheelchair folk. The article featured a photo of Val and Nathan. Val was wearing her *don't mess with me* face. Nathan was smiling and gazing off into the distance. He looked like a happy kid, but it was clear from that photo that he was not going to do any dancing.

So, we took Nathan to the auditions for the opening ceremony of the Games.

When we got to the venue, we joined a long – very long – line of hopefuls, and they came in all shapes and sizes. There were grandparents in baggy tracksuits, adolescents in active-wear and everything in between. There were fit people and unfit people, big people and small people, and there were lots of all of them.

But for a reason we didn't understand – well, we thought we did, we were just wrong about what we thought – we didn't have to wait in line. Though we initially stood in said line, I went to the front of the queue to ask about getting a wheelchair auditioner through the turnstile. The authority that I spoke to asked, 'Is this person Nathan Runyan-Tait?'

I was surprised, and then even more so when she said, 'We've been expecting him, just bring him in through this door over here.' She pointed to a door that was crowd free, met us as we passed through it, and ushered us to a set of seats at the front of the already crowded auditorium. Puzzled but pleased we discussed what had happened for only a short time before a man approached us, sat next to Val and introduced himself to Val and to Nathan. His name was David and he was the Director of the opening and closing ceremonies. We felt like we were talking to royalty. He told us that he was pleased – actually, he used the word *delighted* – that Nathan was auditioning. It might take a while for us to understand what his role would be, but we should please be patient and stick with it.

Shortly after he left, Val and Nathan were called onto the dance floor. They were put at the front of the 50-odd folk that were out there with them. There was a dance instructor on stage in front of them. He gave his audience a short routine they were to follow when the music started. To Val, he called, 'Just improvise. Make it up as best you can.' And, to the rest, he said, 'Okay, folks, here we go. And a one and a two…'

Some of the folk on the dance floor were not that athletic. Others executed the routine with the smoothness of a ballet dancer. Val and Nathan? Well, let's just say that they maintained their enthusiasm through that routine and the additional ones that followed. Val twirled Nathan then twirled herself, then waved Nathan's hands in the air, then did it all again the other way.

After about 15 minutes, Val, Nathan and the rest of that group made way for the next group. Val sat down and wiped a sheen of perspiration from her forehead. Her eyes were shining.

'Nathan enjoyed that,' she said. 'He was smiling all the way through it. Even when we stopped.'

I didn't bother pointing out that he was still smiling, but I did say that I thought she enjoyed it as much as Nathan.

On the way home, we agreed that it didn't really matter if Nathan wasn't selected – in fact we were sure he wouldn't be – because it was a positive and enjoyable experience.

'We tried,' said Val, 'and that's what really matters.'

We were surprised though, the next day, when we got a call from a woman who told us that Nathan had been selected as one of the performers for the opening ceremony.

***

The first rehearsals were held twice a week, and went for four hours in early February, carried out in a hall. In mid-February, they moved to Metricon Stadium, where the actual ceremony was going to be held, meeting twice a week at first, then, from mid-March until the actual opening ceremony, nearly every day. Quite a commitment, and, for Nathan, very tiring.

When they went to the first rehearsal at the stadium, and found their way out onto the stadium ground along with hundreds of other performers, they were singled out by an individual who told them that she was Nathan's Co-ordinator. She would be our go to person for whatever Nathan needed.

Although they were required to attend every rehearsal, they didn't have to be out on the ground the whole time. His co-ordinator took them inside to a private room that had *GC Dancer – Nathan* on the door. Talk about star treatment.

Val explained to the co-ordinator that they needed a hoist, a change table, access to water for cleaning or drinking. Snacks were supplied for Val, and she had access to the green room, however she never went there because it was not very accessible for Nathan.

Over the following six weeks, Metricon Stadium and rehearsals were pretty much all Val and Nathan knew. When they got to the stadium they would go up to Nathan's private room, and wait to see when they were needed out on the ground. When they were called, they entered onto the stadium floor through a corridor that was separate from all the other performers – because it was the only one with wheelchair access from Nathan's room.

In the first few sessions, Nathan was overwhelmed. There was music and movement and people calling – and lots of confusion – and it was too much for the little guy. So, he did what he always did when suffering information overload: he slept. He went to sleep on the way to the stadium, and he slept through the whole rehearsal.

Val's first solution was to turn the music up in the car to blaring. Then when she got him out onto the stadium floor she tugged and pushed and pulled at him to a point where some of the performers must have thought they were in a wrestling match. But, as Nathan could sleep through an earthquake, the blaring music and the wrestling match had limited effect.

We talked to Nathan's GP about it, and he suggested a very *standard procedure* solution. 'Give him a strong short black through his peg just before you leave home,' he said. 'Nathan's metabolism is not that different to everyone else's, so it should perk him up.'

And it did. A strong short black before he left the house, loud music on the way to the stadium, and he made his appearance on the ground with a smile on his face and an eagerness about his person. His enthusiasm was helped somewhat by other performers getting to know him, calling out to him, coming up to him to greet and talk to him.

As time went by, and the dance routines for the performers became a little smoother, then a lot smoother, they worked together until the troupe knew what they were doing, which was when, more excitingly for Nathan, nearly everyone knew his name.

The performance component of the opening ceremony was about two hours long. Nathan's part in it was relatively short, but it did include him holding the Queen's Baton, which was the Commonwealth Games' substitute for the Olympic torch.

As the time of the ceremony drew near, and all the details of how it would unfold were revealed, we found we had a significant problem. In Nathan's role, he was to be on a beach, looking out to sea.

A beach.

Sand.

A wheelchair.

Hmmm!

Of course, Val was not going to let a little problem like that stop them. She found a sympathetic metalworking business that could adapt the axles of Nathan's wheelchair so we could change the wheels. And she searched online and found some tyres that were designed to travel on beaches: large, low-pressure things that wouldn't sink into the sand.

We used an old wheelchair, and the metalworkers designed the axles so the regular narrow wheels could be easily changed to the fat, soft wheels. It still required a bit of oomph for Val to push Nathan and the wheelchair through the sand that was spread across the surface of the stadium, but it wasn't beyond her capabilities.

***

On the night of the ceremony, we didn't need to give Nathan a caffeine hit. He was agog with excitement even before we left the house. He and Val had to be at the stadium two hours before the performance started, so Val had a syringe of super strong coffee just in case, but it wasn't needed. Nathan's excitement stayed on high throughout the drive to the stadium, in his private room with his name on the door, before going down to their entry point. And then it ratcheted up even higher in the corridor at their entry point.

That entry point, you may recall, was selected because it was the only one that was accessible to Nathan's suite. And it was the entry point for the dignitaries, Prime Minister Malcolm Turnbull and Commonwealth Games Chairman Peter Beattie, and the evening's entertainment stars, Delta Goodrem and Ricki Lee. To get to their designated spot, Val and Nathan had to push past the prime minister so close in the very narrow corridor that Val thought they might have run over his toes.

Then, as they waited for the ceremony to start, there was a bit of a kerfuffle behind them as Delta Goodrem came skipping barefooted through the crush to say hi to Nathan.

She hunkered down next to him. Nathan's eyes went wide, and a smile split his face from ear to ear.

'Hi,' she said. 'My name is Delta.'

'Oh, he knows who you are,' said Val. 'He loves your music.'

Delta asked him his name. Val answered for him.

Delta Goodrem talked to Nathan for a few minutes, about the ceremony, about his role, about hers. Nathan was delighted to have her attention, and where I think he was a little in love with her before the meeting, he was absolutely star-struck afterwards.

While we're talking about celebrities, when Nathan finished his performance and was heading back into the corridor, he – quite literally – ran into Ricki Lee, who stayed with him long enough for a photo opp.

As a family member of one of the performers, I had a ticket to the opening ceremony, but I don't remember all that much about it. While Nathan was out on the ground, I kept my binoculars on him. He wore the Commonwealth Games baton uniform, and, with him holding the Queen's Baton, the press cameras focused on him, beaming him all over the world.

After the ceremony the performers went to a club to celebrate. It had been an outstanding success – even the weather behaved – and the mood was positively buoyant. We had hardly walked in the door when the troupe that was most closely associated with Nathan came and took him onto the dance floor. And that was the last we saw of him for a couple of hours.

Well, we did get some short glimpses, when the throng around him swirled and opened just a little, but each time we got a glimpse of him he had a grin on his face and he seemed to be having a damned good time. So, we left him to it, and met up with him again at closing time.

At most of the parties we went to with Nathan, he would sit with us and we would be kind of separated from the rest by Nathan's inability to blend, but this time he was one of the crowd, and they wanted to dance with him, play pool with him, talk to him. Several of them had learned how to communicate with Nate during rehearsals, so they were quite confident to take him away from us and include him in the celebrations.

Chapter 20: Fin

Imagine it. You think one of the most magical events in your life is going to happen, and instead you find your living your worst nightmare. What do you do? You can't run away; you can't change what has happened; you have to learn to live with it; you have to adapt. We've already talked about the processes we went through, the fear, the laughter, tears and frustrations we experienced. But what we haven't talked about is how it changed us.

Our parenthood experiences were not what we planned. If you had asked us before we had Nathan what we would do if we had a child with a disability, we would have said we could not cope. It would be absolutely terrifying. And for a while it was just that. But we woke up from that nightmare. And when we did, we found that we were different.

I have asked myself many, many times, how did Nathan's life change us? We no longer wish that he wasn't disabled, but we do wonder how he shaped us. Are we different because of the life we led with Nathan? Yes. Would we have changed him if we'd had a magic wand? Yes. If we could have taken his disabilities away, of course we would have. Who wouldn't? But he has given us so much, and those gifts far outweigh the regrets.

One of his biggest gifts to us is that we are now emotionally richer and more balanced. He taught us what matters in life, he grounded us, and gave us the ability to sort through the facades and determine what is real and what matters. He taught us to laugh at ourselves. We do of course realise that all children change their parents in some way, and that, if Nathan hadn't had his disabilities, he still would have changed us. But are the changes different because he was disabled? Definitely! And we are happy with what he did for us because – and we are absolutely sure about this – he made us better people. He taught us patience, tolerance and unconditional love.

At a real life *what has happened and what's going to happen next* level, I can say that, unlike most parents' lives, all the Nathan-related disappointments have already happened for us. We had more – way more – than our fair share of them in the early years, but now they are over. Nathan will cause his parents no more disappointments. And that's big. Really big. He never lied to us, got fired from a job, came home drunk, got booked for careless driving, took recreational drugs or got a girl pregnant. There were many more stressful times, many more joys, but no disappointments. We knew what we had. We accepted it. Nothing he did from that point on disappointed us.

***

A quote I read from the father of a disabled child went like this:

> When not interfered with by outside influences, everything nature does, is done with perfection.
>
> Yet my son cannot learn things as other children do. He cannot understand things as other children do.
>
> Where is the natural order of things in my son?
>
> I believe that when a child like mine, who was mentally and physically disabled, comes into the world, an opportunity to realize true human nature presents itself, and it comes in the way other people treat that child.

If this father is right, then the treatment of my son by other people is a strong endorsement of human nature.

Epilogue

Nathan died in September, 2021.

Six months earlier, when he was in hospital, one of the ICU doctors said he was suffering from Chronic Functional Decline.

She then left the room without explaining what that meant. The explanations on the internet didn't clarify it too much, so I called my brother Noel, the surgeon, and asked him to explain it.

Noel has never been one to mince words. 'Do you want the unvarnished version?'

I said I did.

'It means he's dying.'

We took Nathan home. We didn't believe – didn't accept – that he was dying.

He hung on. He Fought. For six months. In that time, we felt like we were watching him on a raft that was drifting further and further away from us. We wanted to reach him, get to him somehow, but we couldn't. We had to just watch while he faded further and further into the distance.

He was home when he passed. It was quick. It was peaceful.

We are grateful for all those things.

We are grateful for the time we had with him.

We are grateful for all that he gave us, for everything he taught us.

We will miss him forever.

In Loving Memory of Robin Tait

Disability Support Organisations

Australian Federation of Disability Organisations
disabilityaustraliahub.com.au/afdo

Autism Aspergers Advocacy Australia
a4.org.au

Brain Injury Australia
braininjuryaustralia.org.au

Brainwave
Brainwave.org.au

Carer Gateway
carergateway.gov.au

Cerebral Palsy Alliance
Cerebralpalsy.org.au

Cerebral Palsy Australia
cpaustralia.com.au

Children and Young People with Disability Australia
cyda.org.au

Council for Intellectual Disability
cid.org.au

Disability Advocacy Network Australia
dana.org.au

Disability Services Australia
dsa.org.au

Epilepsy Foundation Australia
epilepsyfoundation.org.au

Intellectual Disability Rights Service
idrs.org.au

National Disability Insurance Scheme
ndis.gov.au

National Disability Services
nds.org.au

National Ethnic Disability Alliance
neda.org.au

National Mental Health Consumer & Carer Forum
Nmhccf.org.au

People with Disability Australia
pwd.org.au